SENNEN COVE
Lifeboats

SENNEN COVE
Lifeboats

150 Years of Lifesaving

NICHOLAS LEACH

TEMPUS

First published 2003

Tempus Publishing Ltd
The Mill, Brimscombe Port
Stroud, Gloucestershire GL5 2QG
www.tempus-publishing.com

British Library Cataloguing in Publication Data.
A catalogue record for this book is available from the British Library.

ISBN 0 7524 3111 0

Typesetting and origination by Tempus Publishing.
Printed in Great Britain by Midway Colour Print, Wiltshire.

Contents

Preface

The Royal National Lifeboat Institution (RNLI) is justifiably proud of its long history of saving life at sea. The famous hymn by William Whiting, *Eternal Father strong to save*, captures the selfless and gallant spirit of those who risk their lives for no reward to rescue 'those in peril on the sea'. Nowhere is this gallantry and self-lessness more evident than on the coast of Cornwall, where those who crew the county's lifeboats have performed numerous outstanding deeds and courageous acts, many of which are celebrated as part of the region's heritage. At the county's tip lies Land's End, and a mile to the north of this lies the small picturesque village of Sennen Cove, a delightful place on a calm summer day but fearsome when a strong westerly gale blows in from the Atlantic. For one and a half centuries, all those who use the seas off Land's End have been protected by the selfless service given by the lifeboat crew at Sennen Cove, one of the Institution's fourteen stations in Cornwall. The Sennen station, which celebrated its 150th anniversary in 2003, has a proud history since its establishment in the 1850s up to the operation of the station's current modern, fast lifeboats. The 47ft Tyne *Norman Salvesen* and D Class inflatable *Spirit of the ACC*, manned by the volunteer crew, stand ready to help those in diffi-culty off the Land's End coast and put to sea twenty-four hours a day, 365 days a year, in times of need. The station is one of more than 230 managed by the RNLI throughout the United Kingdom and Republic of Ireland and is funded entirely by voluntary contributions.

Acknowledgements

I am privileged to have been asked to write this history of the Sennen Cove lifeboat station, one of the best known of all of Britain's lifeboat stations because of the heroic deeds of its crew and its proximity to Land's End. The station's honorary secretary, John Chappell, was instrumental in getting the book under way and his assistance throughout the project, together with that of Coxswain Terry George, has been invaluable. Tim Stevens, shore helper at Sennen Cove, has also been extremely helpful in providing many photographs, readily answering my queries and freely giving up his time to provide assistance.

I am greatly indebted to the late Grahame Farr whose pioneering research into Cornwall's lifeboat history was of considerable assistance during the preparation of this book. Paul Russell and Jeff Morris assisted with information about services and lifeboats. Brian Wead, Manager of the Service Information Section at RNLI Headquarters in Poole, kindly supplied descriptions of many rescues and Barry Cox, Honorary Librarian at RNLI Headquarters, Poole, assisted with details about nineteenth century happenings at Sennen. Neil Williams, of Cornwall County Council, provided newspaper accounts of some early events.

For supplying photographs for possible inclusion, I am grateful to many people: in particular Phil Weeks, of Chatham, whose excellent painting of the lifeboat *Susan Ashley* hangs in the station's lifeboat house. The following also provided many photographs and their contributions are credited adjacent to the illustrations: Bryan Roberts, of Sennen Cove; Peter Puddiphatt, of Sennen Cove; Paul Richards, of Fowey; Paul Russell, of Hitchin; David Gooch, of Dunstable; Tony Denton, of Shrewsbury; Peter Edey, of Brightlingsea; Derek Harvey, of Mousehole; and Derek King of the RNLI Headquarters, Poole. Finally, on a personal note, my thanks to Sarah for her continued support and patience during my researches.

Nicholas Leach
September 2003

1

Cornwall's early life-savers

A treacherous coast

From Land's End to Lundy Light/A Sailor's grave by day and night

This old couplet provides a succinct description of the mariner's view of Cornwall's coastline which has a reputation amongst seafarers for being one of the most treacherous in Britain. The rugged granite cliffs keep back the sea from Penwith, the old Cornish name for the peninsula, as the county's coasts take the full force of the Atlantic Ocean in the prevailing westerly winds which frequently rise to gale force during the winter months. In navigating the county's coasts, the sailor is presented with many and varied dangers whether he is passing it to go on to other destinations or intending to enter one of the county's ports or harbours. The south coast is characterised by inlets, wide bays, estuaries and natural harbours which can safely accommodate vessels both small and large, while, in contrast, rugged cliffs and rocky outcrops typify the north coast where harbours of reasonable size are few and far between. Of particular fascination to generations of visitors to Cornwall has been Land's End, part of Cornwall's west facing coast. More than a million people visit this granite outcrop each year to gaze out over the sea into the wide Atlantic, over the mythical land of Lyonesse and towards the Isles of Scilly. Few, however, will truly appreciate the natural forces of the sea, wind and tide at this point of the coast.

A mile to the north and at the western tip of the peninsula lies the small village of Sennen Cove, the nearest settlement to Land's End, whose small population grew up relying on the sea for a living. Despite its exposed position, the small harbour at the Cove created beneath the cliff catered at one time for considerable numbers of large boats. They would be hauled up, out of the reach of the tide, and launched through a channel specially cut in the rocks. Throughout the eighteenth and nineteenth centuries the people of the village of Sennen were defined by their relationship with the sea. The boats were employed in pilchard fishing as Sennen was well situated to take advantage of the first annual arrival – usually around the end of July – of this warm-water fish. As well as pilchards, grey mullet and herring also came to the bay, while the shoals and rocks provided a habitat for shellfish which, during the summer season, were caught in pots. Seine fishing for pilchards lasted for four to five months of the year and was both labour and capital intensive in terms of the large boats, the

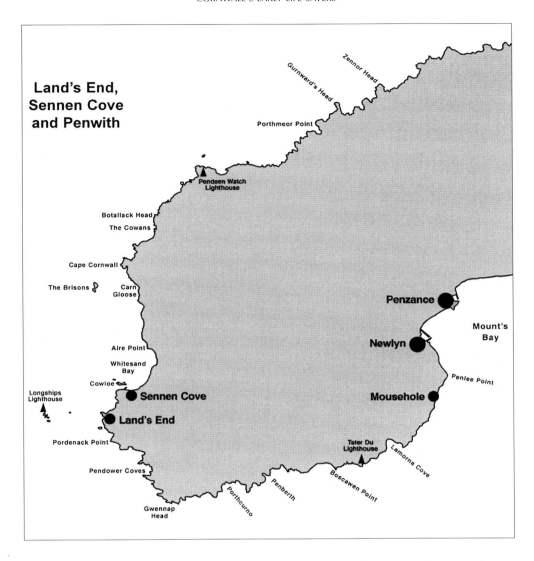

Land's End,
Sennen Cove
and Penwith

shore buildings and the gear. The catch was cured ashore for export from Newlyn to the Latin countries. Seine fishing collapsed after the First World War as motorized drifters operating further afield could reach the shoals before they came into the bays. The autumn herring fishery also came to an end at this time, leaving crab fishing in which more than twenty boats were employed until the outbreak of the Second World War.

The villagers of Sennen have witnessed the demise of many vessels on this treacherous coast. Although in the eighteenth and nineteenth centuries a variety of circumstances contributed to ships being lost, being trapped by bad weather was the most common for wrecked on the Cornish coast. The meeting of different tidal races at Land's End produces confused seas which in times of storms have caught out innumerable craft that ended their days smashed on the granite rocks. This part of the coast offers no safe havens in which to shelter when running from bad weather at sea. When sail was the primary means of power, vessels would make for the safety

Sennen Cove in the late nineteenth century with the lifeboat house just to the left of centre. The circular building near the lifeboat house is the capstan house. (By courtesy of RNLI Sennen Cove)

An aerial view over Sennen Cove taken during the 1990s, looking south, showing the lifeboat house and slipways, the beach car park, the breakwater and the cluster of houses on the clifftops. (Phil Weeks)

of St Ives Bay to the north or Mount's Bay to the south at the slightest indication of a strong wind. Their safety would depend upon knowledge of the best anchorages and the hope that the weather would not change. Within a matter of minutes, a shift in wind direction could turn either bay into a potential death-trap as vessels, caught on a lee shore, were dependent on the strength of their anchor chains for survival. Those craft relying solely on wind power were helpless in the face of storms and gales, and valuable crews and cargoes were often lost through shipwreck. Many were stranded or wrecked through factors often beyond the control of those on board or otherwise involved with the ship as vessels were largely at the mercy of the elements.

General navigation presented many problems, particularly during the eighteenth and nineteenth centuries when inadequate charts would often fail to mark rocks and sandbanks accurately. Negotiating the entrance to a port could also be extremely difficult. Darkness made navigation even more problematical as did fog which, off the western extremity of Cornwall, can suddenly spring up to envelop cliffs and reefs turning them into hidden dangers as the warm air from southern climes meets cold waters. Considering these natural hazards, it is not surprising that wrecks in the area have been many and frequent, creating the need for a lifeboat station in the vicinity. In 1693, a convoy of a hundred ships was caught in a storm shifting westward, forcing the ships to head into the North Channel and causing almost three-quarters of them to be wrecked. In 1703, HMS *Colchester* was wrecked in Whitesand Bay with the loss of about a hundred lives while, between 1823 and 1846, almost 150 vessels were lost between Land's End and Trevose Head. Between Tol Pedn Penwith, south of Land's End, and Gurnard's Head, two-thirds of the way to St Ives, almost the same number of wrecks have been recorded with evidence suggesting that many more occurred but went unrecorded.

Although tales of wreckers luring ships onto rocks with false lights are common, such action was hardly necessary – ships would come ashore without 'help'. One of the most notorious incidents occurred in September 1837 when the ship *Le Landois* grounded in Whitesand Bay near Gribba Point. Her cargo of wines, cordials, cottons, velvet, tobacco and the best brandy was spilled everywhere. The poor country folk in the area soon reached the scene to get what they could. Reports suggest that a drunken and unruly mob of about 4,000 people were faced by twenty-five Coastguards, but only two men were brought to justice as the luxury items from the wreck were soon taken to homes far and wide. The actual extent of wrecking is difficult to prove one way or another, but anyone who could take advantage of an unguarded cargo from a wrecked ship would almost certainly do so.

The first attempts to improve the situation for those at sea involved the construction of lighthouses to effectively mark dangerous points on the coast, coupled with leading lights to guide ships into ports. During the eighteenth and nineteenth centuries many lighthouses were built to improve navigation and today no fewer than four major lighthouses mark the dangerous 'finger' of the Land's End peninsula. Two lie offshore guarding ships from the dangers of hidden reefs – Longships and Wolf Rock – while two more stand on headlands – Pendeen and Lizard – guiding vessels either to the north or south of the peninsula. As well as these static lights, the Sevenstones Lightvessel marks an isolated group of rocks about a mile square in size

almost due west of Sennen Cove and the Tater-Du light indicates a specific danger
spot between Land's End and Penzance.

A lighthouse to mark the Longships Reef, which lies a mile off Land's End, was
first constructed in 1795. The most prominent and western of the rocks which make
up the reef is known as Carn Bras. On this the first lighthouse was built, in 1794-95,
by Lieutenant Henry Smith in conjunction with Trinity House. It was 40ft in height
and stood on the highest part of the rock about 40ft above sea level. Often obscured
by heavy seas breaking over the reef, it was damaged on a number of occasions and,
as a result, Trinity House, which was responsible for its operation and maintenance,
decided to build a bigger tower. The new tower was completed over the course of
three years on a site alongside the first tower and it was first lit in 1883. Although
the station is now operated automatically, until the installation of an electric light, it
was manned by lightkeepers who were relieved by a boatman living in Sennen Cove
where the keepers' families lived in a row of cottages on the cliff top at Land's End.
From the upper windows of these cottages, the keepers' wives would use semaphore
to communicate with their husbands on the lighthouse. In 1974 a helipad was
constructed on the lantern top. Automated in 1988, the light today covers the
Brisons, the inside passage and the Runnelstone Rock and the white light has a range
of nineteen miles.

The Wolf Rock lies just over eight miles to the south and a little to the west of
Land's End and has for centuries been one of the most formidable obstacles to
shipping entering the English Channel. The rock itself is one of the most exposed of
any of the British Isles, receiving a pounding from the Atlantic Ocean in bad weather,
so much so that building a lighthouse on it was impossible until the nineteenth
century when advanced construction techniques, first developed for building a lighthouse on the Eddystone Rock, could be applied. Work on construction of the
granite tower, designed by James Walker, began in 1861, although, prior to this,
several attempts had been made to establish a beacon there. Work continued for more
than eight years until the tower was finally completed on 19 July 1869 and the light
became operational the following year. The tower remains one of the most substantial of any controlled by Trinity House. The diameter at the base is 12.7 metres
tapering to 5.2 metres at the top, the entrance door is made of gun metal weighing
one ton, and in total the tower consists of 3,297 tons of granite.

The lighthouse to the north of Sennen is Pendeen Watch, situated two miles from
Pendeen village. The stretch of coast between Land's End and St Ives is bleak but the
sea lanes are busy, with coasters and fishing vessels frequently passing. Countless ships
have been wrecked upon its rocky shores. The buildings that comprised the new
lighthouse were constructed during 1900 and the light itself was commissioned on
26 September 1900. Originally fitted with an oil lamp, it was connected to the mains
electricity in 1926. Rubble stone coated internally and externally with cement
mortar was used during the construction process. On the southern side of Land's End
is Tater-Du light, which was only established in 1965 to mark the Bucks, a dangerous
rock close under the headland which had previously been marked by a buoy.
However, following the loss of a fishing vessel in poor visibility, Trinity House
decided to supplement the buoy by building a new lighthouse on the cliffs close by.
Further east, on Cornwall's south coast, is the Lizard light, marking the most

Right: An old postcard of Longships lighthouse showing the tower before the helicopter platform, added in 1974, was constructed above the lantern. This tower was constructed in 1875 and was automated in 1988. (By courtesy of Tim Stevens)

Below: Pendeen lighthouse, completed in 1900, is situated on the north coast of the Land's End peninsula. (Tim Stevens)

southerly point of mainland Britain. As early as 1570 a light was considered necessary here, but not until 1751 were any structures built. Alterations made by Trinity House in 1812 left the station much as it is today, with an unused tower close to the operational light.

The first life-savers in Cornwall

Despite improvements in navigation and measures such as the building of lighthouses and beacons as described above, lifeboats on Cornwall's coasts were needed to further improve the safety of ships and their crews, as wrecks remained commonplace. The first lifeboat in Cornwall, stationed at Penzance in 1803, was one of more than thirty boats built by Greathead based on the lifeboat he built for South Shields (at the mouth of the river Tyne) in 1790. This boat, 30ft in length and pulled by ten oars, had a curved keel and double-ended hull. The success of this first lifeboat led to her being adopted as the design upon which most early lifeboats were based, including the first lifeboat in Cornwall. The boat built for operation at Penzance was 27ft in length and 10ft in beam. It cost 150 guineas, of which the insurance company Lloyds contributed £50 while the remainder was made up from subscriptions raised locally. Despite initial enthusiasm, long-term funding and adequate maintenance to keep the boat operational was not forthcoming and she was sold in 1812 never having performed a rescue.

Further attempts to establish lifeboats in Cornwall during the first two decades of the nineteenth century, if indeed there were any, are not recorded. However, in March 1824, at a meeting in London, the Royal National Institution for the Preservation of Life from Shipwreck (commonly referred to as the National Shipwreck Institution or NSI) was established to be responsible for 'the preservation of lives and property from shipwreck' on a nationwide basis. This encompassed the funding, building, operation, maintenance and organization of lifeboats and lifeboat stations. Initially quite successful, the new organization added to the number of lifeboats in operation in Cornwall, including one at St Mary's (Isles of Scilly). However, local initiatives tended to prevail in the county and lifeboats built for Padstow in 1827 and for Bude a decade later were both funded and operated locally. A lifeboat for Sennen Cove was not considered at this time.

After initially being quite successful in increasing the number of lifeboats around the country, by the 1840s the organization's efforts started to falter through lack of funds. The Institution found raising money for lifeboats difficult and enjoyed only limited success in providing a nationwide lifeboat service. Its annual income dwindled during the 1830s and 1840s until, by 1850, with no public appeals made for over a decade, the level of finance available to the Committee of Management was at its lowest level. Improvements were essential if life-saving work around the coasts was to continue but without funds this was impossible. On 2 May 1851, Algernon, Duke of Northumberland, was appointed president and through his energy and efforts during the 1850s, working alongside the secretary Richard Lewis, much-needed improvements to the Institution were implemented.

In 1851, the Duke produced a report which contained a survey of the lifeboat stations then in existence around the coast with a brief description of life-saving facilities at each. In the entries for Cornwall the report highlights the need for a lifeboat at Sennen by stating: 'Lifeboat much wanted here. It will be placed forthwith by the NSI.' Renamed the Royal National Lifeboat Institution (RNLI), the organization began to make new public appeals for finance. A new design of lifeboat, the self-righter, was developed and, with greater funds available to it, the newly-reformed Institution was able to increase lifeboat provision throughout the country. In Cornwall, many new stations were established. Apart from the lifeboat provided for Sennen, stations at Bude, Penzance (both in 1853) and Padstow (in 1856) all received new lifeboats as provision was made to cover the most notorious danger spots off the county's coastline.

The lifeboat station at Sennen Cove was established as the direct result of a shipwreck that occurred in January 1851 and which, as well as drawing attention to the need for a lifeboat in the area, resulted in one of the most heroic rescues ever undertaken in Cornwall. Early in the morning of 11 January 1851, in thick fog, the 250-ton two-masted brig *New Commercial*, of Whitby, struck the Brisons, a pair of rocks about a mile south-west of Cape Cornwall, and broke up immediately. The crew of nine, together with the master's wife, reached a ledge on the rock from where they were seen at daybreak. However, because of the high seas, nothing could be done to assist them. Matters worsened when, at about 9 a.m., a large wave washed them off the ledge and all but three drowned. One of the survivors, Isaac Williams, contrived to leave the rock on a portion of floating wreck and, assisted by the tide, managed to get clear of the Brisons and into Whitesand Bay where he was picked up by the small boat *Grace* that had been launched by William Roberts with four other Sennen fishermen.

Meanwhile, the other two left on the rock, Captain and Mrs Sanderson, remained on the Little Brison. Throughout the afternoon of 11 January further attempts were made to reach the stranded couple. Captain George Davies, RN, Inspecting Commander of the Coastguard at Penzance, ordered the revenue cutter *Sylvia* to come round from Penzance and up to Land's End whilst he, with Lieut Maxey, RN, of the Sennen Coastguard, and a Pendeen man took up positions on Cape Cornwall. *Sylvia* courageously made her way round the Longships, being completely hidden at times by flying spray. As they came abreast of the Cape, Mr Forward launched a boat from the cutter and with four men tried to get near the rock but failed and was lucky to regain the safety of the cutter. As daylight was failing and nothing more could be done until the next day, the rescuers reluctantly halted their efforts.

By the following morning, 12 January, hundreds of people thronged the cliffs to watch no fewer than six vessels approach the rock and attempt to affect a rescue. With daylight the wind veered a little to the south-east which caused the seas to abate. Four boats came from Sennen, one manned by the Coastguard and the other three by local fishermen. Captain Davies arrived in charge of a Preventative boat from Pendeen, whilst the cutter's own boat was again launched under the charge of Thomas Forward, Commander of the Revenue Cutter. They were cheered as they attempted to reach the Brisons but the sea was so high that no boat could venture to within a hundred yards. However, Captain George Davies, Inspecting Commander of the Coastguard at Penzance, who was in one of the boats on the scene, had brought several nine-pounder Dennett rockets. Although this rocket had never been tried here before, either on land or from a boat, it was the only chance to successfully rescue the two survivors on the rock who were by now in a terrible condition. The danger to Davies of firing the rocket from his boat, with a line attached, was considerable but he decided it was the best hope. The printed instructions stated that the person firing should be several feet to the rear to avoid danger, but this advice was to be ignored.

Gunner Selby volunteered for the task, but Captain Davies decided to attempt the firing himself. He put his crew in a Sennen boat, fixed the triangle in position, placed another boat astern to train his own and fired the rocket. Although he was enveloped in flame, he sustained no injury. The first line fell short into the sea after being cut on a jagged edge but the second reached the rock and landed close to the master on the Little Brison. Captain Sanderson fastened it around his wife's waist and she then jumped into the sea with the line attached and was pulled to the waiting rescue boat. Despite surviving a rapid succession of huge waves that broke over the rocks just as the line had been attached, she died of exhaustion before reaching the shore. The master was pulled into another boat, after which all were safely landed at Sennen. The bodies of Mrs Sanderson and several members of the crew were later buried in the churchyard.

For the outstanding effort made in trying to undertake a rescue throughout the two days, Captain Davies, who became Inspector of Lifeboats soon afterwards, and Thomas Randall Forward, Commander of the cutter *Sylvia,* were both awarded the RNLI's Gold medal. Silver medals went to various other men involved as follows: Charles S. Carr, Gunner from the Revenue Cutter, James Richards, William Surrey, Henry Jones and Henry Richards, Mariners from the Cutter, James Ward, First Class Boy from the Cutter, James Burne, Thomas Kerley, Robert Eastaway, William Henry Selley, boatmen of the Sennen Coastguard. Other awards were made to the Sennen boatmen who had put out in the atrocious conditions to help, including William Roberts and the four men of *Grace,* Samuel Nicholas and the four men of *Two Brothers,* both of whom had taken their craft out from the Cove to assist if possible.

The presentation of medals to reward acts of outstanding bravery performed by lifeboat crews and meritorious actions by anyone saving lives at sea had been introduced at the same time as the National Institution was founded. The idea was first suggested by the Institution's founder, Sir William Hillary, who believed that a medal or badge 'might have a very powerful effect (in inducing men) to render their utmost aid to the shipwrecked of every land, in the moment of their extreme distress.' The Gold and Silver medals were introduced at the founding meeting of the Institution and the first medals for gallantry awarded at a meeting of the Institution's Committee of Management on 10 July 1825. The Bronze medal was not instituted until 1917.

A lifeboat for Land's End

The impetus for the establishment of a lifeboat station at Sennen had been provided by the wreck of *New Commercial* and, with the backing of the National Institution, steps were taken to turn the need for a lifeboat into reality. In July 1851 an order was placed for a small, light self-righter, one of the first to James Peake's design, built by Wallis, of Blackwall; she was 21ft in length, 6ft 6in in breadth, and rowing eight oars. Peake was Master Shipwright of the Royal Naval Dockyard, Woolwich, who, under the instructions of the Institution, modified the design of James Beeching. The Peake-designed self-righter was altered and improved over time and eventually became the accepted standard throughout the country.

At the Annual General Meeting of the RNLI held on 22 April 1852 it was reported that a new lifeboat was 'to be sent to the station ... to be managed by local committee in acknowledgement of the gallant conduct of the Coast Guards and fishermen of that place on the occasion of the wreck of the ship *New Commercial* on the Brisons'. Whether this refers to the boat ordered in 1851 is not clear because this boat was in fact never sent to the station. Despite being ready in October 1851, trials showed her to be unsatisfactory, although in what way is not recorded. Notwithstanding the various alterations made to try to improve her, she was condemned and later broken up having never been used on the coast. As a result, another boat had to be built and, in January 1853, Forrestt, of Limehouse, was ordered to construct a lifeboat which was allocated to the station. At the RNLI's next Annual General Meeting in April 1853 the boat destined for Sennen was reported as being under construction, 'to be ready in May'. In *The Lifeboat*[1] of May 1852, detailed particulars of the new boat were provided: she was 25ft in length, 6ft 8in in breadth, had a depth amidships of 3ft 2in and was fitted with a keel 20ft 6in long; she had four thwarts, was rowed by six oars, was fitted with six six-inch delivering tubes, weighed 28cwt and her sheer of gunwale was 2ft; her displacement at load-water line, with crew and stores, was 45cwt and she carried 5cwt of iron ballast and 3cwt of cork ballast; she was built to Peake's design and was of clench construction from elm. She was completed satisfactorily at Forrestt's yard, passing her survey by the RNLI's Inspector in June 1853.

The first Sennen Cove lifeboat arrived at the village early the following month having been sent via Penzance, where she arrived on a British & Irish Steam Packet Co. steamer, and was then towed to her station by a Revenue cruiser. Preparations at Sennen for the new lifeboat involved the construction of a new stone boathouse measuring 28ft by 12ft which stood on the site of the present boathouse. This house, built during the year previous to the boat's arrival, had been funded by James Trembath, of Mayon House. Although the boat satisfactorily completed her trials at the station, launching soon proved to be somewhat difficult and so in 1856 a carriage was ordered from Boydell & Glasier to improve matters. It was drawn by eight horses supplied by Mr Phillips of Mayon Farm and took the lifeboat along the Cove road to launch from Whitesand beach. Meanwhile, not only did he fund the new house, Trembath also undertook the

---

[1] *The Lifeboat* is the official journal of the RNLI and was first published in 1852.

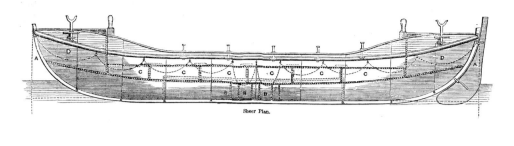

Sheer Plan.

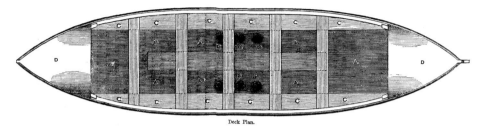

Deck Plan.

Diagram of the Peake-type self-righting lifeboat as used by the RNLI from the 1850s: Sennen Cove's first lifeboat would have been built along similar lines. (From *The Lifeboat* journal)

management of the station and became the first honorary secretary responsible for the station's operation.

Throughout her time at the station, the first lifeboat remained unnamed. Her only service took place on 6 and 7 May 1856. She set out to bring the abandoned barque *Charles Adolphe*, of La Rochelle, into Penzance, towing the casualty with the help of four other small boats. The vessel had been in collision in a south-east gale off Land's End. As a result of this service, £100 salvage money was awarded to the Sennen lifeboat for her part in saving the vessel. After a fifth had been deducted for the maintenance of the boat, in accordance with the Institution's rules, the eight lifeboatman received between £8 and £9 each. Although this amount considerably exceeded the normal £1 service money, the local secretary, James Trembath, appealed to the Institution that this was less than the men in the other boats received. However, the Institution pointed out that the lifeboatmen had not incurred risk to their own lives or property during the service and so no additional payment was forthcoming.

The lifeboat of 1853 served at Sennen for just over a decade but, although it did not perform any further rescues, the crew did assemble on 20 December 1862 during a gale after reports that an unknown vessel was in difficulty. No launch took place and within two years a new lifeboat was on station. The new boat arrived in July 1864 and at 33ft in length was larger than her predecessor. She was conveyed from her London-based builder Forrestt, of Limehouse, to Penzance by the Great Western, Bristol and Exeter, South Devon and Cornwall, and West Cornwall Railway Companies. She was then towed round to her station by a revenue-cruiser by permission of the Controller-general of the Coastguard. Funded by a gift from Mrs Mary Ann Davis, of Bideford, she was named *Cousins William and Mary Ann of Bideford*. In order to accommodate the new lifeboat, the boathouse was enlarged at a cost of £80 5s 0d. In commenting on her arrival, *The Lifeboat* of 1 October 1864 stated 'she has given great satisfaction to her crew. As the coast here is exposed to the great swell that sets in from the Atlantic ocean, which falls in huge breakers on the shores, a boat of the finest description is required'.

Cousins William and Mary Ann of Bideford performed two effective services while at Sennen. The first took place on 13 October 1865 when she put off after signals of distress had been fired from the Longships lighthouse. On reaching the lighthouse the crew found that one of the lightkeepers was seriously ill and so he was brought ashore. On 25 May 1866 the crew assembled with a view to assisting the brig *Helen*, of Aberystwyth, and other vessels in distress in Whitesand Bay in a strong east-south-easterly gale but in the end no launch was undertaken as it was deemed unnecessary.

The second effective service was an outstanding rescue which resulted in formal awards being made to those involved. During the afternoon of 23 October 1868, the government lighter *Devon* was making her way round Land's End while en route to Queenstown (now Cobh) in Ireland from Devonport, loaded with stores. She was strongly built and a good sea boat and could probably have weathered the hard gale blowing. However, during the evening her officers mistook her position and in the dark ran her stern onto the Brisons. Despite the efforts of the master and crew to avoid the inevitable disaster, the ship began sinking almost as soon as she struck the rocks. Her boats were lowered but almost immediately swept away and the vessel itself began breaking up. Of the eighteen on board, seventeen, including the Captain, a woman and two children, were drowned. Only the mate, a man named George Davis, survived the buffeting among the rocks and wreckage and succeeded reaching a cleft on the Little Brison. The Coastguards on Cape Cornwall saw the wreck early in the morning of 24 October and, although at first nothing could be seen on the island, when it became clear someone was still alive the lifeboat was called. Coxswain Matthew Nicholas assembled the crew and the lifeboat was launched, soon reaching the rock on which the survivor had been reported. The lifeboatmen spent almost an hour shouting to attract the attention of the survivor, repeating their efforts several times during lulls in the storm. However, since no reply was received, and nobody was found, so the lifeboatman headed for the shore again. But just as they were leaving the scene, Davis moved his position and was seen. He immediately wanted to swim to the lifeboat but with so many rocks to contend with was stopped from doing so by his rescuers. Sylvester Morrison, of the Coastguard at Sennen, had joined the lifeboat crew with his rocket apparatus. They anchored about 180 yards to leeward of the rocks. The stand for the rocket quay was found to be too high so it was lashed fore and aft in the lifeboat. The first line that was fired went over the rock near Davis and he managed to haul it in, albeit slowly as he was so weak from his ordeal. He was then able to haul a buoy over and in this was himself hauled into the lifeboat, 'half insensible with cold and exposure' as the report in *The Lifeboat* explained. In recognition of their efforts during this outstanding service, Coxswain Nicholas and Chief Officer Sylvester Morrison were awarded Silver medals.

Between these two services, *Cousins William and Mary Ann of Bideford* was involved in a notable gathering of Cornish lifeboats on 10 September 1867 at Penzance to mark the opening of the new public buildings in the town. The lifeboats from

A LIFE-BOAT RACE IN 1867.

From a print in the possession of Mr. J. E. Hooper, Hon. Secretary of the Natural History Museum and Antiquarian Society of Penzance.   The race was in Mount's Bay, Cornwall, between the Life-boats stationed at St. Ives, Sennen, Penzance, Porthleven, Hayle and Mullion, and took place at the Inaugural Ceremony of the new Mullion Life-boat *Daniel J. Draper*, built out of a fund raised by the *Methodist Recorder* in memory of the Rev. D. J. Draper, who was drowned in the wreck of the *London* in the Bay of Biscay.

Contemporary line drawing showing various Cornish lifeboats at Penzance on 10 September 1867 for the naming of the Mullion lifeboat and a keenly-contested race, which was won by the Sennen lifeboat *Cousins William and Mary Ann of Bideford*.

Penzance, St Ives, Hayle and the new Mullion boat, which was christened and launched the same day, were drawn through the streets on their carriages in procession by teams of horses. The boats were decked with ribbons, evergreens and flowers and the crews completed the scene wearing cork life-jackets. Over ten thousand people assembled on the Western Estplanade to witness the launch of the new Mullion boat after she had been named *D.J. Draper* by the Mayoress. As she entered the water, the Porthleven and Sennen lifeboats were ready to greet her and their crews cheered in salute of the new boat. When all six lifeboats were afloat, a hard-fought rowing contest took place which the Sennen lifeboat won, with the Penzance lifeboat *Richard Lewis* coming second and the Hayle boat *Isis* third.

2

The later pulling lifeboats

Denzil and Maria Onslow

The lifeboat at Sennen had clearly proved its worth during the rescue of October 1865 but, although *Cousins William and Mary Ann of Bideford* served for a further twelve years at the station, she did not perform any more effective services. In April 1880, after receiving damage, she was taken by sea to Penzance for repairs, and it was decided that a new lifeboat would be better than the old one repaired. In August 1880 *The Lifeboat* reported that, as 'The lifeboat met extensive damage at different times,' a new one had been ordered for the station. The new boat, funded by a gift from Miss Maria Onslow, of Staughton House, St Neot's, who had donated £300 to the RNLI, was named *Denzil and Maria Onslow* in memory of the donor's late brother and cost a total of £363 to build. She was a standard 34ft self-righter, pulling ten oars double-banked. Her public inauguration took place on 20 August 1880 at Penzance, when the annual swimming races were being held at the town. The boat's self-righting qualities were put to the test during the day and a friendly race was organized between the new Sennen boat and the Penzance lifeboat *Richard Lewis*, 'to the great satisfaction of the large assemblage of spectators' as the *Cornish Telegraph* stated in its account of events.

During her time at Sennen, *Denzil and Maria Onslow* was launched five times on service and is credited with saving ten lives. She only performed two life-saving rescues the first of which took place on 9 January 1883. At 1.30 p.m. that day, the cutter *Spring*, of Guernsey, bound from Swansea for Dinn with coal, was seen showing a signal of distress. The lifeboat was launched and, on reaching the casualty, found that she had been run into by a schooner. The cutter's jib boom and part of her stem had been severely damaged and, as a result, she was leaking very badly. Two lifeboatmen, together with Chief Officer Steed of the Coastguard, who was in charge of the lifeboat in the absence of the regular coxswain, boarded the casualty and assisted in anchoring her safely. The cutter's crew of three were then landed by the lifeboat.

The other life-saving rescue by *Denzil and Maria Onslow* took place on 15 October 1889. The steamship *Malta*, bound for Liverpool from Italy with passengers and a general cargo, went ashore at Wheal Castle, about four miles from Sennen, in dense fog during the evening. At 8.30 p.m. the lifeboat was launched and found that the

Model of *Denzil and Maria Onslow*, the station's second lifeboat. Although the mast's position within the boat is incorrect, the model gives a good idea of the size and form of the standard self-righter of the late nineteenth century deployed throughout the British Isles.

passengers had been landed so stood by at the master's request. At 6 a.m. the following day an attempt was made to tow the steamship off the rocks but this was unsuccessful and, as a result, the steamer became a total wreck. Before leaving, the lifeboat took off the master and six of the crew who were still on board, with the rest of the crew landing in the ship's boats. Although a routine service for the lifeboat, others involved received formal recognition by the RNLI: at a meeting of the Institution's Committee of Management on 14 November 1889, the Thanks of the Institution inscribed on Vellum was accorded to Edmund and William Roberts of St Just for their help in landing passengers from the stranded steamship. A reward of £5 was also given to two men for saving, at considerable risk, six of seven men who were in one of *Malta*'s boats which had been capsized by an enormous wave as it returned to the shore with salved property in a strong north-westerly wind.

After the *Malta* incident, *Denzil and Maria Onslow* was called on again a few more times, but did not perform any effective services. She was launched on 30 September 1891 in a strong gale and rough seas after signals had been seen from the Longships light-house indicating that a schooner was in distress. The crew assembled at the lifeboat house but when Coxswain Matthew Nicholas arrived, several of the men refused to go out in those conditions. The Coxswain called for volunteers: seven of the normal crew of thirteen came forward together with five others, mostly holiday visitors. This hastily-assembled crew then launched the lifeboat and proceeded to sea. They could see the schooner's flares off the Brisons but, by the time the lifeboat reached the spot, no trace of the casualty could be found. They searched for two hours, by which time the wind had increased to hurricane force preventing a return to Sennen. So the boat made for St Ives, which was reached after four hours of hard rowing. Three of the holiday visitors who had volunteered to make up the crew, Frank Bodilly, barrister; Thomas L. Burgwin, stockbroker; and Harry J. Welch, artist, were accorded the Thanks of the Institution inscribed on Vellum for their courageous action. It later transpired that the vessel, *Annie Davies*, of Carmarthen, had been found abandoned the following day in the Bristol Channel by the steamship *Gazelle*, the crew having taken to the boats which were swamped in the gale.

Ann Newbon

In June 1892, *Denzil and Maria Onslow* was sent back to the RNLI's London storeyard for examination where it was found that, after thirteen years on station, she was in an unserviceable condition. A month later it was announced that she was to be broken up, so a new lifeboat was ordered for the station. The new boat, named *Ann Newbon*, was provided from the legacy of Robert Alger Newbon, of Islington, London, and was sent to her station on 20 July 1893 by rail, arriving at Penzance three days later. A standard 35ft self-righter, she had been built by Woolfe at Shadwell, London. The drop keel with which she was fitted improved her seaworthiness particularly when sailing and, according to *The Cornishman*, she was also 'noteworthy for the big air chambers, fore and aft'. Although she was seen at the time as a great improvement over the previous boat, with a displacement of less than four tons, a beam of little more than 8ft and power provided by ten oarsmen, it is hard to imagine the new lifeboat, or even her predecessor, coping in the heavy seas often experienced off Land's End. But she did cope and went on to gain an outstanding service record, which is a great credit to those who manned her. In fact, she proved to be considerably more in demand than previous Sennen lifeboats and, during almost three decades on station, is credited with launching seventy-five times on service and saving well over a hundred lives.

Within a year of the arrival of the new boat, a new lifeboat house was constructed to accommodate her. The previous lifeboat house, constructed in 1875 at a cost of £258, was on the landward side of the road leading to the harbour and was too small for the new boat. The new house was built in an attempt to overcome the difficulties in launching that had persisted since the first lifeboat had been stationed at Sennen, and which are discussed in more detail below.

The new lifeboat's first service took place on 24 December 1894 after HMS *Lynx* had struck sunken rocks off Sennen Cove in a dense fog at about 8 p.m. She successfully got off the rocks, anchored in deep water and, at her commander's request, the lifeboat stood by throughout the night. When the fog had cleared by about 5.30 a.m. the following day, Christmas Day, the lifeboat crew helped to raise the warship's anchor as her capstan had been carried away. *Lynx* then proceeded with *Ann Newbon* in tow and the Coxswain piloting for twelve miles eastward along the south coast. As the warship was not leaking as badly as was first thought, she proceeded to Devonport Naval Dockyard for repairs and the lifeboat returned to her station.

On 17 October 1895, *Ann Newbon* launched at about 5 p.m. to the steamship *Harberton*, of London, which was bound from the capital to Barry, in ballast. The steamship had stranded on Jibben Bean, part of the Kettle's Bottom Reef between the Longships and Land's End. It was just high water when she struck and, as the tide ebbed, she was firmly aground on the rocks. At low water she was high and dry and in danger of slipping off into deep water. The crew launched the boats but, by taking their personal belongings with them, overloaded the boats so they were in danger of capsizing. Once the lifeboat was on the scene, she was asked to stand by and remained on hand throughout the night with the ship's boats attached. At 5 a.m. the steamer drifted off with the rising tide, damaging her propeller in the process and lying helpless among the rocks. However, under the direction of the Coxswain, she was

Ann Newbon, a 35ft self-righting type which served the station for almost thirty years. This photograph shows the crew wearing standard issue cork life-jackets and the boat ready to be launched. The man with the white collar standing on the beach by the stern is Colonel T.H. Cornish, honorary secretary of the station from 1886 until his death in 1931. Coxswain Henry Nicholas can be seen on board the lifeboat, at the stern, in white trousers. (Bryan Roberts, by courtesy of RNLI Sennen Cove)

anchored in a safe place until a steam tug arrived. With a lifeboatman on board acting as pilot, the tug was able to get close enough to the casualty to attach a rope. The steamer was then towed into Whitesand Bay where she was anchored at about 8 a.m. and *Ann Newbon* returned to her station.

The next service took place on 9 November 1898 after the 1883-built schooner-rigged steamship *Bluejacket*, of Cardiff, bound from Plymouth for her home port in ballast, with a crew of twenty-two, struck hard and fast on the rocks under the Longships lighthouse in clear weather. The Assistant Coxswain was fishing off Cape Cornwall when his attention was drawn to signals from the lighthouse. He immediately returned to Sennen, informed the Coxswain of what he had seen and, at 1.05 p.m., *Ann Newbon* was launched. The lifeboatman reached the scene of the wreck within twenty minutes of the crew mustering and found that four of the steamer's boats had already been launched. One of these had been stove in and two contained the men's personal belongings. It was decided to land the crew and so the laden boats were towed back to Sennen where they arrived after three hours of strong pulling against a very strong tide. The steamer, owned by the Bluejacket Steamship Co. of Cardiff, later became a total wreck.

In 1901, *Ann Newbon* undertook two services within the space of a month. On 21 October three fishing boats appeared to be in trouble as night fell and, at 8.30 p.m. one moored a mile offshore. The crew signalled for help and so the lifeboat was launched and brought ashore the two men from the boat. At 10 p.m. another fishing boat arrived at the moorings and signalled for help, so the lifeboat put out again and landed the three occupants of the fishing boat. The lifeboatmen stood by to help the third boat which arrived about midnight but, by then, the sea had subsided so the lifeboat was not needed.

On 18 November the lifeboat undertook the second service of the year when she launched at 4.15 p.m. in heavy seas and a strong north-westerly gale to the schooner *Mary James*, of Penzance, which was bound from Newlyn for Swansea with copper ore and stone. Her masts and sails had been broken, her bulwarks had been carried away and her decks were almost awash. A steamship was standing by but could not help the schooner which was gradually drifting towards a dangerous lee shore. However, *Ann Newbon* was able to get alongside and save the schooner's crew of six.

A routine service in dense fog was then undertaken on 27 May 1902 after the torpedo boat destroyer HMS *Recruit* had struck rocks half a mile north of Cape Cornwall at 4 a.m. The Coxswain was alerted by the destroyer's distress flares and *Ann Newbon* was launched at once. She stood by the casualty until tugs arrived to help refloat the vessel. During the afternoon, after the destroyer had got off the rocks, she was towed to Penzance and the lifeboatmen returned to their station at 5 p.m.

On 4 February 1903 *Ann Newbon* undertook a long and arduous service which tested the stamina of her crew. The steamship *Berwick*, of Newcastle, had become a total wreck after getting stranded on the Runnelstone in a strong south-westerly breeze and rough seas. She was spotted by the Coastguard soon after 7 a.m. and the Coxswain was informed. The lifeboat was quickly launched and found the steamship's Captain and four men in a small boat standing near the wreck which, in the meantime, had drifted close to the cliffs. The five men were taken on board the lifeboat which was then rowed towards Penzance in search of another small boat in which were the other men from the steamship who had left the casualty soon after it had gone aground. As these men had landed safely, the lifeboat was unable to find them, but she went on to Penzance where the five men taken from the first boat were landed at 11 a.m. After ascertaining that their assistance was no longer required, the lifeboatmen on board *Ann Newbon* left Penzance at 12.30 p.m.,

The 1883-built steamship *Bluejacket*, of Cardiff, stranded on the rocks under the Longships lighthouse on 9 November 1898. *Ann Newbon* launched to her aid and brought ashore the whole crew. (Gibson of Scilly)

arriving back at Sennen at 8 p.m. having been away from their station for more than twelve hours.

Less than a month later, the unfortunate wreck of the barque *Luna* occurred off Land's End. The vessel, of steel construction and 800 registered tons, was on passage from New Zealand to Liverpool with a general cargo when she got into difficulty off Pendeen in a north-west-by-west gale losing part of her mast and head gear. The Coastguard kept a watch on the disabled vessel but did nothing until they saw distress signals. Only when within four miles of land were rockets fired and flares set alight indicating she was in difficulty. The *Cornish Echo* of 6 March 1903 takes up the story:

> It was very evident to the men on the watch that the barque was in an almost hopeless condition. They however did all they could to render assistance to the crew, acquainted the Sennen lifeboat crew, and proceeded to Cape Cornwall with the rocket apparatus. On arrival, they were informed that the vessel had struck the Brisons, the spot where it was feared she would come to grief, and where no aid could reach her ... As soon as the vessel struck she went down and was broken to matchwood in less than ten minutes. The violence of the storm and the sea gave the men no chance of life ... Nothing could be done, only wreckage washed ashore would give a clue to the name of the lost vessel and the extent of the loss of life.

During the search for further wreckage, two men, both from Penzance, were drowned. Meanwhile, on the shores of St Just five bodies were found and wreckage

The crew of *Ann Newbon* in 1912. From left to right, back row: James Howard Nicholas, Thomas Nicholas, -?-, Herbert Nicholas, Jimmy Nicholas, Edward (Teddie) Nicholas. Front row: Henry George, Bowman John Penrose, Coxswain Thomas Henry Nicholas, Second Coxswain John White Pender, and retired Coxswain Henry Nicholas. (By courtesy of Bryan Roberts)

was washed up, most of which was identified as belonging to the wrecked barque. At the inquest on the bodies of five of those drowned, Coxswain Henry Nicholas gave evidence regarding the failure of the lifeboat to launch to the barque's aid. He explained that the lifeboat dare not go nearer than three-quarters of a mile of the Brisons when the weather is gale force. He added that, if they had received the alarm before the ship had struck, the lifeboat could have reached the ship before she was driven on to the rocks and probably saved the crew. The Coastguard, though they saw the vessel in distress, could not call the lifeboatmen until they saw the ship showing signals of distress. The coroner hoped that in future this regulation would be relaxed while the jury returned a verdict of accidental drowning on the five victims.

More than five years elapsed before *Ann Newbon* was next called upon. However, when she was needed in December 1908, the service undertaken resulted in the awarding of a medal to her Coxswain. At 9 p.m. on 28 December the Coxswain received a telephone message from Tol Pedn signal station that a large ship was riding at anchor close to the shore in Porthcurno Bay, with heavy seas running and a southerly gale. *Ann Newbon* was launched but within half a mile of the Longships the crew found that making headway against the overpowering strength of the wind and sea was impossible. They returned to Sennen only to launch again at 3 a.m., as the wind had shifted. They had not gone far before the wind again changed, this time to west-south-west, causing the seas to become more violent. The darkness had made the launch more difficult for the Coxswain who could not even distinguish the men in the boat, while heavy rain further reduced visibility. The wind was so strong that, from the lighthouse at Porthcurno Bay, the lifeboatmen closely reefed the fore sail while the following seas swept over the lifeboat often filling her to the gunwale.

When daylight broke, the lifeboatmen found themselves to be half-a-mile-south of the Runnelstone Buoy. The Coxswain hauled the boat to windward and made for Porthcurno Bay, bringing her alongside the ship. The vessel, *Fairport*, of Liverpool, in ballast, was lying broadside to the beach in heavy breaking water with her sides rolling under and she was so close to the shore that she bumped at low water. As the anchors were holding, the master, Captain W.A. Armstrong, asked the lifeboat just to stand by. At about 9 a.m. the weather moderated slightly and the tug *Blazer* arrived on the scene. However, the seas were breaking so hard over the ship that the tug could not approach close enough to be of assistance. At the Captain's request, the lifeboat took to the tug the line which initially proved too short. The lifeboatmen, however, added lifelines from the lifeboat until eventually they were able to make a connection of sufficient length. Soon afterwards, *Fairport* slipped her anchors and was successfully towed away by a tug as the lifeboat made for her station. As the wind and sea were too heavy to recover, the lifeboat headed for Penzance where she arrived at 1.10 p.m. The Newlyn lifeboat had been launched at 11 p.m. but failed to find the casualty. For his efforts during this fine service, Coxswain Henry Nicholas received the RNLI's Silver medal; during this service, the crew was made up of second Coxswain Nicholas, Matthew Nicholas, Robert Pender, J. Nicholas, J.W. Pender, T. Pender, Philip George, J.P. George, J.H. George and Edward Nicholas, all of whose efforts were recognised.

During the early hours of 13 March 1910 the Coastguard reported flares off Porthcurno, close to the shore. *Ann Newbon* launched and, on approaching the spot, her crew saw a second flare which had been fired from a small boat in which were four men. They were the crew of the Brixham trawler *Harry* that had become stranded on her way to the fishing grounds and rapidly become a wreck. The lifeboat towed the small boat back to Sennen through a heavy gale, arriving at the Cove at 9 a.m.

In 1912 *Ann Newbon* performed two services in quick succession. The first, on 29 February, was to the steamship *Northlands*, of Cardiff. She stood by as the Newlyn lifeboat, *Elizabeth and Blanche*, assisted to save the vessel. The second service, only a fortnight later, also saw her standing by a stranded ship. On 14 March, at about 8 p.m., the Coastguard reported that a sailing vessel was in a dangerous position near Land's End in a light south-westerly breeze but heavy seas. *Ann Newbon* launched and went to the south side of Land's End where the lifeboatmen found the trawler *Condor*, of Brixham, anchored within fifty yards of the rocks. The trawler's master asked the Coxswain to stand by and the lifeboat remained at hand until 2 a.m. By then the tide had slackened and the wind shifted to the north-west so the trawler was able to get clear and the lifeboat returned to station.

In a moderate east-north-easterly gale and rough seas on 4 April 1913, the ketch *Woolwich Infant*, of Falmouth, parted her cable and drifted rapidly towards the Cowloe Rocks. *Ann Newbon* was launched after signals of distress from the ketch had been seen. By the time the lifeboat arrived on the scene, the ketch's crew had dropped a second anchor which fortunately held the ketch in a position just short of the rocks. The lifeboat stood by until about 12.30 p.m. when, as the ketch was riding safely, she left. At about 3 p.m. a signal was made from the ketch that the lifeboat was required again. However, before *Ann Newbon* reached the ketch again, its crew had been taken off by a shore boat. The ketch subsequently went ashore and became a total loss.

On 14 August 1913 the steamship *J. Duncan*, of Cardiff, bound from Cardiff for Devonport with coal, was stranded in thick fog at Tol Pedn Penwith and was spotted in difficulty at about 7 a.m. As soon as reports of her demise reached the village, the crew mustered and *Ann Newbon* was launched. Although the lifeboat's help was refused by the captain, the lifeboat stood by throughout the day in case she was required. At about 5.30 p.m. the captain decided to abandon ship and so the lifeboat came to his aid. Two of the steamer's crew jumped into the lifeboat while the rest took to the ship's three boats which were towed by the lifeboat to Porthgwarra Cove, where they were beached.

When war broke out in the summer of 1914, Sennen Cove's lifeboat station was in a good state of health: the boat and its gear were in good repair, the boathouse and slipway had benefited from continuous improvements over the previous two decades or so, and the launching site was protected by a newly-constructed break-water. Although many lifeboat crews were called upon to perform heroic acts of bravery during the war, undertaking rescues while negotiating minefields and without the aid of coastal lights, the main problem for Sennen was the availability of sufficient men, should the lifeboat be required for service. By March 1916 this had become an important issue but, despite the fact that many lifeboatmen joined up, Lt Edward D. Drury, EN, District Inspector for the Western District, reported after his annual visit to the station that sufficient numbers to make up a crew were obtainable. However, by October 1917 the situation had changed: Coxswain

Nicholas was able to raise a crew but only just, as two more men had been called up. In order to make up the full crew he relied on men who were away fishing but who would return for the winter. When the war ended in November 1918, the manning problems had worsened as, although a crew could be raised, most were elderly and few helpers were available. The District Inspector doubted whether a low water launch in rough sea would be possible but better times were ahead in terms of crewing.

The demands on *Ann Newbon* during the First World War were somewhat infrequent until 1917, when she performed three services, carried out efficiently despite the manning problems. The first, on 20 February 1917, was to a seaplane that was seen to be in difficulties just outside the breakers. The lifeboat was able to save the only occupant in a moderate breeze and heavy seas and a naval patrol boat later removed the plane. The next service took place in April. At 9.30 p.m. on 19 April the lifeboat was launched to the steamship *Polyktor*, of Ithaca, laden with coal, which had gone ashore off Pendeen. The steamer's captain asked the Coxswain to stand by and, at about 3 a.m. on 20 April, she floated off and drifted towards the shore. The anchors were let go but she sank at daybreak so the Captain and six others were taken on board the lifeboat. The remaining crew of twenty-one got ashore in the ship's boats. The third and final service of the year took place on 10 September. *Ann Newbon* was launched at 6.40 a.m. that day in fine weather to the steamship *Ioanna*, of London, which had been torpedoed by a submarine off the Longships. Already in attendance was a patrol boat which had taken off some of the crew. The lifeboat took off two wounded men and a boy and brought them ashore.

The final service by *Ann Newbon* during the war took place on 7 February 1918 after the steamship *Beaumaris* had been torpedoed just over two miles north-by-west

The steamship *J. Duncan*, of Cardiff, with a cargo of coal, stranded at Tol Pedn Penwith on 14 August 1913 with *Ann Newbon* standing by, to the right. (Gibson of Scilly)

of the Longships. The lifeboat was launched to help as the steamer was coming towards the shore and the lifeboatmen piloted her in until she grounded. Some lifeboatmen then went on board to help let go the anchors, as the Captain and Wireless Operator were the only persons then left on board. The rest of the crew, eighteen in total, were in a boat about two miles out. The lifeboat then set out to search for this boat and soon found it, returning those on board to safety. Meanwhile, the Captain had been landed by shore boat but he and his engineers were taken back to the steamer by the lifeboat, which then stood by until her services were no longer needed.

During 1919, *Ann Newbon* was involved in three outstanding services, the first of which took place on 17 March after the Falmouth steamer *Falmouth Castle* had struck the Lee Ore Reef, an underwater granite pinnacle off Tol Pedn between the Runnelstone and Land's End. The motor fishing drifter *Ben-Ma-Chree*, whilst on her way to the fishing grounds from Newlyn, encountered a boat from the steamer in which were seven men who were saved using the drifter's small boat manned by the drifter's master and two of its crew. The steamer was beached in Porthcurno Bay by her Captain and news of the stranding soon reached Sennen. The lifeboat was immediately launched through a very heavy ground sea in a light wind and the lifeboatmen found the steamer ashore. The seven men on the fishing boat were transferred aboard the lifeboat which landed them at Penzance. The rest of the crew were taken off by Porthcurno's rocket apparatus whilst the Captain's wife, aged sixty-eight and in a state of considerable distress, was saved by Alfred Jackson, of Porthgwarra, in his 14ft punt. Jackson affected the rescue with considerable difficulty amid the heavy seas, which were breaking right over the wreck, but he managed to land the woman safely. His efforts were recognised by the RNLI with the award of the Silver medal. The three who manned the drifter's small boat, Thomas Hicks, the drifter's master, Edward Sleeman and David Sleeman, jnr, were awarded Bronze medals by the RNLI.

The second service of 1919 took place on 29 April when *Ann Newbon* was launched into a rough sea and a north-north-easterly gale to the steamship *Frisia,* of Rotterdam, which was bound from Cardiff for Rouen with a cargo of coal. The steamer was seen north-west of the Brisons with a severe list and her bridge in the water. During the evening, the steamer drifted rapidly toward the shore and, when about half a mile north-west of Aire Point, she foundered and her crew of fourteen left in their boat. The lifeboat was only 200 yards away as the steamer foundered and so she took its crew on board and safely landed them at Sennen.

The final service of 1919 proved to be the most outstanding rescue performed by the Sennen lifeboatmen in *Ann Newbon.* On 29 November three naval motor launches left Queenstown for Southampton escorted by a destroyer to be paid off. During the night the wind gradually increased, blowing from the south-south-west, so that by the morning gale-force conditions prevailed. One of the launches was towed by the destroyer, but the other two were under their own power. In the severe weather all were shipping water and by mid-morning, as a result of this, the engines of ML.378 stopped as the vessels were off the Land's End. The destroyer was some way ahead, but the other craft, ML.173, got a rope to her sister and began a tow. The first rope parted so a new one was attached. However, soon this parted too and the disabled launch was left adrift less than a mile from the Longships Reef. In this perilous position, she fired minute guns and the alarm was soon raised. *Ann Newbon* was launched and quickly reached the scene. Meanwhile the launch's nine-man crew, wearing life jackets, had taken to their small dinghy as the last hope, but immediately this small boat capsized throwing the men into the water. Four of them were able to regain the motor launch which itself was then flung onto the rocks, leaving them stranded. The lifeboatmen witnessed these events and, after anchoring the lifeboat as close to the stranded men as possible, veered their boat down to the five struggling men in the water. They were just in time to save four of the men but the fifth, the second in command, unfortunately drowned. The lifeboatman then turned their attention to the four men on the rocks, half buried by water and frozen, as the launch had disintegrated and disappeared already. The lifeboat's anchor was raised and the lifeboat was carefully manoeuvred through a gap in the rocks. The anchor was again dropped and the four men on the rocks were then dragged through the water by ropes to the safety of the lifeboat.

The lifeboatmen had taken a tremendous risk, particularly during the last stages of the operation, for the slightest mistake would have wrecked the lifeboat on the reef and her crew would have had virtually no chance of rescue. In appreciation of the gallantry and skill displayed, the RNLI awarded its Silver medal to Coxswain Thomas Henry Nicholas (61) and Second Coxswain Thomas Pender (27). Bronze medals were awarded to the remainder of the crew: E. Nicholas (40), J. Nicholas (40), H. Nicholas (34), Edmund George (27), R. Roberts (15), T. George (11), J. Penrose (7), H. Nicholas jnr (6), Edward George (6), Ernest George (6), Herbert Nicholas (2), J. H. Nicholas (1). The numbers in brackets indicate how many times each man had been out on service in the lifeboat. The awards were presented by Sir Clifford Cory, Bt, MP for St Ives Division, on 10 April 1920.

Ann Newbon performed her last three services during 1920 and 1921, all of which were routine in nature. On 22 September 1920, a boat was reported wrecked on Longships Reef in a moderate north-easterly gale. After launching, the lifeboat found the motor fishing boat *Our Boys*, of Porthleven, which had struck the south rock, but had drifted away leaving her crew of five stranded on the rocks. The lifeboat took them off and landed them safely, while the fishing boat was salvaged later. On 22 January 1921, the lifeboat crew were called out at 11 a.m. by the Coastguard after a steamer had been seen at anchor about two miles south of Runnelstone firing signals of distress. The lifeboat was launched and found the steamship *Haliartus*, of Liverpool, returning from Antwerp in ballast, caught in a moderate westerly gale and heavy seas. Her tail shaft was broken and so the lifeboat stood by until a salvage steamer came to tow the casualty to Mount's Bay. The final service undertaken by *Ann Newbon* occurred on 16 August 1921. The barge *Strumble*, of London, parted from her tug in a moderate westerly breeze and rough seas and began drifting towards Longships Reef. The lifeboat was launched and took the barge in tow but the wind and tide proved to be too strong. After the barge had passed through a channel in the reef, the lifeboat caught up with her again, and two lifeboatmen were put on board. The lifeboat was then able to hold the barge in position until the tug could reconnect the tow.

Getting the boat afloat

The rugged nature of the coast at Land's End presented considerable difficulties for those attempting to launch the lifeboat at Sennen Cove and getting the boat away from the beach for many of the rescues described above was often extremely difficult. Indeed, getting any boat afloat in the face of the predominant westerly winds could be a physically demanding undertaking. Since the establishment of the lifeboat station in 1853, gradual improvements to the launching procedure have been introduced as some unusual and innovative solutions to the problem of getting the boat afloat have been tried. This section will discuss those attempts and describe each solution.

Launching from the first lifeboat house, built in 1852 (described above), involved dragging the lifeboat over skids down the foreshore and manhandling it into the sea. As this situation was somewhat unsatisfactory, a launching carriage was sent to the station in 1855 but this only partially improved matters. In 1864, although a new lifeboat house was ordered to be built for the lifeboat newly arrived at the station, repairs to the existing one costing just over £80 proved a satisfactory and more economical option. However, the problems of launch and recovery continued, highlighted by an accident on 5 April 1871 when the lifeboat *Cousins William and Mary Ann of Bideford* was launched on her quarterly exercise. A report in the *Cornish Telegraph* described what happened: 'The launching of the boat, and working of the crew, were highly satisfactory, but on pulling the boat up the slip after the drill, when almost at the top, the chain broke. She slid down the slip, and coming in contact with a small boat belonging to a fisherman, crushed its side.' The accuracy of these events was corrected in a subsequent edition of the newspaper by Michael Bazeley, Resident Engineer of Trinity House at Penzance, who explained that the accident was the result of negligence by those employed in hauling the lifeboat back to her boathouse and the chain had not in fact broken. The chain had been removed after the boat had been hauled almost to the top of the slipway but before the blocks had been put in place to hold her there. When the chain was removed, as Bazeley explained, 'the boat having nothing to hold her, ran down and caused not only the damage mentioned but also considerable injury to herself'. Bazeley had felt obliged to correct the original account and exonerate Trinity House because the chain belonged to Trinity works at Sennen. That nobody was injured or killed on this occasion was probably more down to luck than judgement, although the incident highlighted the difficulties as well as the dangers of the launch and recovery procedure at Sennen and the fact a more efficient and safer system was needed. However, no improvements to launching were forthcoming.

In February 1874 temporary repairs had to be made to the boathouse to ensure it was usable until the expiry of the lease. At the same time, Captain J.R. Ward RN, the RNLI's Inspector, paid a visit to the station during which he was urged by the honorary secretary to authorise the construction of a new house as the existing one was in such poor condition it was on the point of falling down. The Institution leased a new site from John Symons, of Mayon House, Sennen, for twenty-one years with the cost of one shilling per annum, agreed if Symons was handed the present house. As this arrangement was deemed satisfactory, plans for a new house on the new site were put in hand. Trounson's tender of £250 for the construction work was accepted in June 1874 and the new building was completed by the end of the year. It still stands on the landward side of the main road, opposite the current lifeboat house, now used as a small souvenir shop. The construction of a slipway for launching – arguably more important than the house itself – took longer and was still not complete by November 1876 so a new builder, S. Lugg, was engaged. For an additional £19, the access road and launching slipway were finished the following year, with the land and materials being provided free of charge by Symons. These further improvements to both the road and slipway made the launching easier but did not represent a long-term solution and the problems continued. By June 1879 the lifeboat had been damaged on three occasions due to the narrowness and steepness of the slipway and rocks often obstructed the launching path. Less than a year later, further damage to the boat resulted in her being deemed unsuitable for service and a replacement vessel was ordered.

During the 1880s, the Sennen lifeboat performed only two effective services suggesting that launching the boat may have been problematic. However, although no record exists of particular problems with the boathouse or slipway at this time, it would appear that the house of 1875-76 was as unsatisfactory as the one it had replaced. One improvement was implemented in September 1890 when the RNLI provided £5 towards a lantern to guide the fishermen into harbour from the south and west. By July 1892, because space in the house was so tight, the lifeboat was kept on the bed of her carriage without wheels. The RNLI's Committee of Management insisted that she be kept on the carriage, which had been in use for twelve years. Although the issue remained unresolved, it highlighted the inadequacy of the boathouse. In order to improve matters and also because the old lifeboat had become unfit for further service and was to be broken up, the crew's request for a 35ft by 8ft 3in ten-oared lifeboat fitted with one drop keel was approved in October 1892.

The new, larger lifeboat would need to be accommodated in a new, larger house and so on 26 January 1893 the RNLI's District Inspector for the Western District, Commander T.H. Willoughby-Beddoes, and Mr Small, the Borough Surveyor, investigated the best site for a new lifeboat house. Only two places were found where launching was possible, one of which was in such a bad state that it was too dangerous to even consider. The other was found to be satisfactory except at low water spring tides when, for about an hour and a half each side of low water, exposed rocks presented an obstacle. Despite this preliminary visit, no immediate decision was taken about a new house so when, in July 1893, the new lifeboat, *Ann Newbon*, arrived on station she had to use the 1875-76 house regardless of its unsuitability. However, the need for improvements was not forgotten: in November 1893 Willoughby-Beddoes recommended 'a complete alteration' to the station 'when the opportunity occurs'. Finally, in February 1894 a new carriage built by Bristol Wagon Works was sent, via the Great Western Railway (the old carriage was sold locally). However, this seems to have made little difference and launching continued to prove difficult.

A month after the new carriage had been delivered, the RNLI's Engineer & Architect, W.T. Douglass, visited the station and concluded that a radical solution was needed: the only way to overcome the launching difficulties was to build a completely new house and slipway. Ambitious plans were drawn up with the intention that the lifeboat could be rapidly launched at all states of the tide. Douglass suggested that the present lifeboat house could be exchanged for the old lifeboat house – then in use as a fishermen's shelter – and the materials in the old house reused in a new building. He estimated that the work would cost approximately £1,470 including £1,350 for the building of the boathouse and slipway. The considerable cost of the work delayed the Institution's decision to commit to the project because, despite these proposals, nothing further was done in 1894 except the laying down of permanent skids and the removal of boulders at the foot of the slipway at a cost of £120.

However, the impetus to improve the fabric of the station gained momentum in March 1895 when the RNLI's Chief Inspector visited. He 'consider[ed] the launching arrangements more difficult and dangerous than at any station in the United Kingdom' and stated that the station was a particularly important one as it covered about thirty-five miles of coast. He immediately recommended that a new house and slipway be built as soon as a lease and the Board of Trade's permission had been obtained. He also emphasized that the road leading to Whitesand Bay had be repaired and a slip made over the boulders at the foot of the beach. By June 1896 his recommendations were being acted upon. Douglass had again visited the station and his designs for a new boathouse, slipway and carriage house, together with improvements to the roadway to Whitesand Bay, were approved by the Committee of Management. In October 1895, the lease of the site had been agreed and work on the new building began.

By the summer of 1896 the extensive new boathouse, the new carriage house and the slipway were ready, built at a total cost of £1,680. A road so that the lifeboat

A view over the bay looking towards the lifeboat house and slipway, with the eastern slipway in the foreground via which the lifeboat could be launched using her carriage if necessary. The roadway was constructed at the same time as the lifeboat house. (By courtesy of Bryan Roberts)

The lifeboat house built in 1894-96 seen from the rear, with the carriage house to the right and doors at the rear to bring the lifeboat out, should the need arise. (By courtesy of Bryan Roberts)

could be taken northwards by carriage towards Whitesand Bay had been completed for an additional £325. The station used the slipway when the tide was in and employed the carriage, which was housed in a small store beside the boathouse, for low water launching. The new house had sliding doors which could be opened in the face of a gale when hinged doors had proved difficult to manhandle. Doors at both ends of the house enabled the boat to be taken out from the rear if necessary and haul it onto the carriage for a carriage launch. In 1904 the carriage was removed as it had not been used since the construction of the new slipway.

While the new house improved the efficient operation of the station, it was by no means perfect and the difficulties in launching and recovering over the relatively exposed beach remained. The lack of shelter became apparent when, in May 1894, Commander Willoughby-Beddoes, District Inspector for the Western District, took the lifeboat out on exercise in heavy seas but, as the boat returned, she had to be laid off for some time while the crew watched for an opportunity to safely beach her. In his report to the RNLI's Committee of Management, Willoughby-Beddoes described the considerable risk to both lifeboat and crew in these circumstances and suggested that the small breakwater be raised and extended. However, the matter was not pursued any further at this time, probably because of the considerable expenditure on the new house.

In November 1900, T.H. Cornish, the station's honorary secretary, suggested that a new breakwater should be built and stated it would cost £2,200. Not only would it aid the fishermen in launching and recovering their boats, but it would also greatly help the lifeboat at times when severe weather conditions made launching impossible. Although Cornish was backed up by the local committee, the RNLI's Committee of Management would not pursue the matter as the breakwater was not the Institution's responsibility.

A further five years passed before the matter was raised again when events proved that Cornish's suggestions showed considerable foresight. Had they been acted upon, a tragic loss of life – that eventually led to the breakwater being improved – might

The lifeboat house of 1894-96 from the rear, after the rear doors had been bricked up. The stern and rudder of the lifeboat, probably *Ann Newbon*, can just be seen at the far side of the house. (By courtesy of Bryan Roberts)

have been averted. As it was, the events of March 1905 proved that a sheltered launching site was essential by highlighting the problems of putting to sea in the face of a gale.

On 14 March 1905, the iron full-rigged ship *Khyber*, of Liverpool, of 2,025 gross tons, built in Liverpool in 1880, homeward bound from Melbourne in Australia, was caught in a severe gale as she approached the Cornish coast. She was seen by the keepers of the Wolf Rock lighthouse, on course for the Lizard in the face of a freshening south-westerly wind. By the time she anchored off Land's End, her boats had been washed away and her crew had taken to the rigging. As dusk fell, she was slowly being driven into Mount's Bay and towards the shore. Both anchors were let go off Guthensbras Point whilst she was only a hundred yards or so from the cliffs. The anchors held until about 7.10 a.m. on the following day when, with the gale as strong as ever, the ship struck the rocks at Porthloe Cove, near Tol Pedn Penwith and Porthgwarra and, within ten minutes, broke in half amidships. Her mizzen mast collapsed, followed by the fore and main masts, and her crew were flung into the sea. Only three of the twenty-six on board escaped with their lives and were helped to safety by those who had been watching from the shore.

Unfortunately the rockets and signals for assistance fired from the ship during the night were not seen by anyone on the shore or at the lighthouses. Only at daybreak did news of the ship's plight spread throughout the small communities around the bay. A message reached Sennen at 6.30 a.m. and the lifeboat and rocket brigade were mobilized. However, launching the lifeboat proved to be impossible in the conditions, with the seas 'head on', according to a contemporary account, while large boulders from the small breakwater thrown across the slipway by the gale blocked the launchway. The carriage, which had been removed the previous year having been deemed unnecessary, might have enabled the boat to launch, but of course was not available. Meanwhile, despite the best efforts of many of the Cove's inhabitants, the rocket apparatus arrived at the scene too late. The Penzance lifeboat made a gallant attempt to save the *Khyber's* crew but was unable to sail to the scene of the wreck. The salvage steamer *Lady of the Isles* towed the lifeboat to Porthloe arriving at about 11 a.m. only to find the vessel had already foundered. The bodies of the ship's captain, Henry Rothery, and twenty-two of his crew are buried beside the tower of St Levan Church.

A formal Board of Trade Inquiry into the whole incident was held at Penzance Town Hall between 26 and 28 May 1905 under the chairmanship of Colonel Henry Willey Williams of St Ives, assisted by two local Justices of the Peace, Rear-Admiral John Ferris and others. No blame was attached to the lifeboat's crew, who were commended for their efforts in trying to launch. However, attention was drawn to the fact that 'improvements are required to enable the Sennen lifeboat to be launched in all weathers and at any state of the tide' noting that the channel was blocked meaning that 'the lifeboat and its gear, which are in good order [with] an excellent crew, ... is almost useless owing to the difficulty in launching'. The Inquiry recommended that a breakwater be built to protect the launching site at Sennen. As a result of the *Khyber* incident, Colonel Williams devoted himself to getting the work completed and opened a private subscription to raise the necessary funds, although finding the money and then undertaking the construction work proved to be a rather protracted business. Having already collected £1,200, in May 1906 he sought financial support from the RNLI who supplied the £250 requested. By February 1908, tenders for the work had been obtained but the total cost had increased and an

Looking up the beach to the lifeboat house of 1894-96. This photograph was probably taken in May 1922 after the arrival of the station's first motor lifeboat, *The Newbons*. Her bow can be seen inside the lifeboat house, while her predecessor, *Ann Newbon*, is hauled up beside the house. The house has been extended at the front to accommodate the new lifeboat. (By courtesy of Bryan Roberts)

The breakwater and slipway seen in the 1920s, when the railway for trolley launching was in use. (By courtesy of Bryan Roberts)

additional grant of £50 was made by the RNLI to enable the work to be completed. A year later, work on removing the old breakwater began and, by the end of 1909, the new breakwater had been completed greatly easing the problems of launching the lifeboat, particularly when compared to the early years of the station's existence. The total cost of the breakwater was approximately £4,000, made up by local subscriptions with £1,000 given by the government as well as the RNLI's contribution.

The breakwater soon proved its worth to the lifeboatmen and fishermen at the Cove. In February 1914 the lifeboat was exercised in the worst conditions possible for getting to sea but safely got away from the beach after a long pull against the north-westerly gale before sail could be set. Despite the improvements made since the 1890s, the local committee was still not satisfied and, in July 1914, stated that the station should be 'first class, so a new and larger lifeboat should be supplied and the slipway should be reconstituted. Until a motor lifeboat was sent, the station was not suitably equipped.' Although motor lifeboats had, by this time, become operational at several stations around the British Isles, the outbreak of war in 1914 and the consequent reduction in available resources severely delayed the RNLI's fleet modernization programme and thus the construction of further motor lifeboats. The war also meant that the shoreworks needed before a motor lifeboat could be stationed at the Cove had to be postponed.

The process of stationing a motor lifeboat at Sennen began in November 1914 when the area's District Inspector, Lt Edward Drury, visited the station to discuss the local committee's request for a motor lifeboat. He stated that, before a motor lifeboat could be sent, further improvements to the launching system were required but, as the cost of constructing a slipway was too great, he suggested a trolley and rail system. At most slipway stations, such as that at nearby Penlee Point, the slipway's gradient was sufficiently steep to carry the boat into the water using gravity alone. At Sennen, however, a long and relatively flat slipway would be required to get the boat to a suitable point for it to float and so the trolley and rail was seen as the best solution.

Soon after the Inspector's visit, a deputation including the Inspector, the Coxswain, Thomas H. Nicholas, and retired Coxswain Henry Nicholas visited the lifeboat station at Hilbre Island in Cheshire to inspect the launching arrangements there. At Hilbre the boat was kept on a trolley which went down rails laid over a slipway and those who saw it were suitably impressed so it was decided that this method would be appropriate for Sennen.

Further discussions about the future plans for the station were held with assurances sought from the Harbour Authorities that the breakwater would be adequately maintained. In 1915, once these assurances had been received, the RNLI decided that a motor lifeboat would definitely be provided for the station. In March 1916 an estimate for building the new launching facilities put the cost at £3,700. This included alterations to the boathouse, the construction of a drop keel pit, building a loft for the motor mechanic's workshop, provision and fixing of winch and petrol engines, lengthening the slipway, alteration of gradient and laying the trolleyway, excavation of rock and provision of a turntable and trolley. At this point, the RNLI's Committee of Management, whilst approving the scheme in principle, decided not to commence the work until the war was over.

With the end of the war, the improvements were soon put in hand and, during 1919, extensive alterations were made to get the station ready for the new motor lifeboat. A slipway with railway tracks was constructed, together with a short recovery slip at the top of which was a turntable outside the boathouse. Launching was achieved using this new and unusual arrangement by a trolley which went down the rails on the slipway. When it reached the end of the track, buffers stopped the trolley while the boat's momentum forced it into the water. During this period, the RNLI was building slipways where possible to launch lifeboats as this method of launching had a number of distinct advantages over the carriage launch. Firstly, it was considerably faster as removal of the pin holding the boat at the top was all that was required to get the boat away; secondly, the use of a slipway enabled a heavier lifeboat to be operated and the new motor lifeboats were generally larger and heavier than their pulling counterparts.

The actual construction of the slipway and extension of the boathouse at Sennen was not an easy or cheap undertaking. Not only did it involve construction of a new boathouse, but loose boulders 180ft beyond the end of the proposed slipway had to

The plaque marking the construction of the breakwater in 1908. (Tim Stevens)

THIS STONE WAS PLACED HERE BY THE FISHERMEN OF THE COVE TO REMIND FUTURE GENERATIONS THAT THIS BREAKWATER WAS BUILT BY PUBLIC SUBSCRIPTIONS RAISED BY THE UNTIRING EFFORTS OF COLONEL H. W. WILLIAMS OF ST IVES, J.P. TO WHOM AND TO ALL SUBSCRIBERS THE COVERS OWE A GREAT DEBT OF GRATITUDE. JULY, 1908.

The foreshore at Sennen showing the lifeboat house after the alterations of 1919 made for the first motor lifeboat. (From an old postcard supplied by Derek Harvey)

be removed creating a channel that was 3ft deep at low water spring tides, 35ft wide along its length with sufficient water available to steer the lifeboat to open water at all states of the tide. By September 1919 the work on excavating the channel as well as building the trolleyway, supplied by Messrs J. Lisaght of Bristol at a cost of £412, was under way but the total cost of the project had risen to £5,100. In November 1919 the engineers stopped for the winter as bad weather prevented further progress with the trolley way. They resumed work in January 1920 and made good progress. In March 1920, additional expenditure of £80 for lengthening the boathouse and £200 for altering the trolley was approved. A month later, a further additional expenditure of £2,000 over and above the £5,636 already approved was sanctioned as a result of a rise in the price of both labour and materials. Costs went on rising until a five figure sum had been spent by the RNLI in readying the station for the new motor lifeboat. The report of the naming ceremony of the new boat, *The Newbons,* which took place in August 1924, stated that:

> Besides the cost of the boat, it had cost the institution £11,000 to provide a suitable boathouse and launching slipway. It was expensive, but there was one item in the Institution's expenditure which was never curtailed – The money spent on the Boats and their gear. The Institution asked its men to face the sea at its worst and cruellest moments, and because of that it was not content to give them anything less than the best that care and money could provide.

However, despite such expenditure at the station, the trolley and railway system did not last long as it proved somewhat unsuitable. Although pleased with the new lifeboat, the coxswain and crew soon became disappointed with the launching arrangements.

In theory, the lifeboat was supposed to slide into the water when the carriage hit the buffers at the end of the track. In practice, however, this rarely happened. Because of the shallow gradient of the slipway, the lifeboat's momentum was often not great enough to carry her off the carriage. On such occasions, the task of then getting the twelve-ton boat afloat was considerable. Even when she did come off, if the trolley's speed was insufficient the boat could be damaged before getting away. In October 1925 the coxswain told the Branch Committee that he would have to resign unless new arrangements for launching were introduced.

Action was swift. The trolley was abandoned and between 1927 and 1929 the station was entirely reconstructed. For part of this time the lifeboat was off service. The finished station consisted of two slipways – a long launching slipway and a shorter hauling-up slip with a turntable at the head for transferring the boat from one to the other. The new launching slipway was a massive construction, starting from a higher point than the top of the old railway with a gradient of about one in nine. The smaller slipway was of equally sturdy construction but its shorter length meant that its toe was well within the protection of the breakwater. Before recovery was possible, the lifeboat might, on occasions, have to wait for the tide but the shelter provided by the breakwater ensured this could be accomplished in comparatively calm conditions. Within the boathouse, the turntable meant that, after rehousing, the lifeboat could be turned to face the launching slipway. This arrangement meant that the boat could be recovered bow first unlike at most slipway-launched stations where, with only one slipway, a stern first recovery has to be employed.

Because the new boathouse had to accommodate the circle for the turntable, upon which the lifeboat could be turned through 360 degrees, the finished building was of enormous proportions. On the seaward side of the road through the village, it

The lifeboat house was rebuilt in 1927-29 with the turntable inside making its dimensions enormous. The 1894-96 house was extended seaward and northward, a new roof was built and two slipways for launching and recovering the lifeboat were introduced. This somewhat extravagant arrangement has remained to the present, albeit with alterations for subsequent lifeboats. (By courtesy of Bryan Roberts)

The lifeboat house and slipways of 1927-29 photographed in 1995 after the house had been converted for the 12m Mersey. (Nicholas Leach)

The substantial lifeboat house constructed in 1927-29 with a gable-ended roof. The small fishing boats pulled up on the beach have been a common sight at the Cove for more than a century and a half. (Nicholas Leach)

dominated the surrounding buildings and provided an impressive sight for first time visitors to the area. Despite its size, the building provided little in the way of facilities for the lifeboatman, particularly compared to modern boathouses built since the 1990s. A small committee room was partitioned off in one corner and a mechanic's workshop was also provided. However, despite these significant improvements to the launching arrangements, the boat still could not be launched an hour and a half either side of low water, while rehousing was also sometimes not possible during certain states of tide or weather. Only with the modern era has a truly effective launch and recovery system evolved, as described below.

3

The first powered lifeboats

Powered by an engine, the next lifeboat at Sennen Cove was significantly different from her predecessors. The introduction of motor power to lifeboats in the form of the internal combustion engine was a significant advance. Although crews in the pulling and sailing lifeboats often performed remarkable and extraordinary feats of life-saving, a powered lifeboat provided distinct advantages over one relying on sails and oars. It had a greater range, could make headway against the wind more easily and provided greater manoeuvrability when near a casualty. During the first decade of the twentieth century the RNLI began to develop motor lifeboats and, in 1904, an existing lifeboat, the 1893-built *J. McConnell Hussey* from Folkestone, was fitted with a 2-stroke Fay & Bowen petrol engine which gave her a speed of approximately six knots. This first motor lifeboat then went on trials at a number of stations, including Newhaven and Tynemouth, where she proved quite a success.

However, many technical problems had to be overcome in order to successfully operate an engine on board a lifeboat. These included keeping the engine dry, even in the event of a capsize, ensuring it was totally reliable both when starting and when running, keeping the propellers it was driving free from damage. As the problems were gradually surmounted, lifeboats powered by the internal combustion engine began to be built. Further lifeboats were converted to motor during the 1900s and, as the RNLI's engineers gained confidence and experience with the new technology, the first purpose-built motor lifeboats were completed in 1908. By the end of the first decade of the twentieth century, the first tentative steps towards motor lifeboat design having been taken, motor power was becoming a vital element in life-saving at sea.

Further advances in technology were delayed by the First World War but, once this was over, the RNLI made up for lost time by embarking upon an ambitious building programme. The first motor lifeboats in Cornwall were stationed at the Lizard in 1918 and at St Mary's in 1919 and, during the years between the two world wars, motor lifeboats were sent to ten of Cornwall's lifeboat stations including, of course, the important station at Sennen Cove. The decision to station a motor lifeboat at Sennen had been taken during the war. Indeed, as early as December 1914, the RNLI's Chief Inspector, Commander Thomas Holmes RN, suggested that a 38ft by 9ft 9in motor self-righter, similar to the Newhaven lifeboat, should be placed at the station. Almost six years later, in April 1920, the Committee, Coxswains and crew accepted a 40ft motor self-righter, slightly longer than that originally offered.

The Newbons

The first motor lifeboat to serve at Sennen Cove arrived in May 1922 and seems to have been an almost instant success with her crew. During the trials with the first motor lifeboats in 1904 and 1905, many of the crews who saw the powered boats at first hand were sceptical about their capabilities and particularly suspicious of the benefits an engine would bring. However, by the time a new motor lifeboat had been allocated to Sennen Cove, such prejudices seem to have been overcome because, in a Return of Service dated September 1921, the Coxswain, Thomas Pender, stated: 'Don't delay the new boat.' While *Ann Newbon* had given sturdy service to the station, an improved craft was both required and wanted at the Cove.

Sennen's first motor lifeboat, 40ft in length, 10ft 6in in beam, fitted with a single 45hp Tylor JB.4 four-cylinder, six-stroke petrol engine, was of the self-righting type, built along the same lines as a pulling and sailing lifeboat but fitted with an engine. A number of boats of this 40ft self-righting type were built by the RNLI during the 1920s and all provided good service at the stations they served. On trials the Sennen boat reached a maximum speed of just over seven knots with the engine developing 885rpm. She carried a total of sixty gallons of fuel which gave her a radius of action of almost fifty miles. The new lifeboat was completed in 1922 at the East Cowes boatyard of J. Samuel White at a cost of £8,622 4s 9d. She was, like her predecessor at the station, provided from the legacy of Robert Alger Newbon, of 275 Upper Street, Islington, London. From the sale of stock, he had left about £18,000 to the RNLI, which was to be used to provide five lifeboats for the English coast to commemorate Ann, Betsy, Lucy, Nancy and Bob Newbon. The motor lifeboat funded from this money was named *The Newbons* and replaced the five pulling and sailing lifeboats (including that at Sennen) which had carried the individual names. *The Newbons* arrived on 1 May 1922 after a three-day journey from Cowes in company with the new Appledore lifeboat *V.C.S.* (ON.675), another 40ft motor self-righter. The lifeboats had left Cowes on 28 April under the command of Captain Harold G. Innes RN, Inspector of Lifeboats for the Western District, and covered the 226 miles in thirty hours at an average speed of seven and a half knots.

The new lifeboat was named at a ceremony on 29 August 1924. She was presented to the Branch by the Hon. George Colville, Deputy Chairman of the Committee of Management, on behalf of the RNLI. In making the presentation, the contribution made by the donor to the RNLI was recalled by Mr Colville as recorded in the November 1924 edition of *The Lifeboat*:

> Through the generosity of the late Mr R.A. Newbon, no fewer than five Pulling and Sailing Life-boats had been built and endowed, each bearing the name of a member of his family. One of them for many years had been stationed at Sennen Cove. All these five Boats had now been withdrawn, and one Motor Lifeboat had been built and endowed in place of four of them.

The new boat was received on behalf of the Branch by Mr G.B. Hicks and, after she had been dedicated by Revd Trevor Lewis, Sub-Dean of Truro Cathedral, she

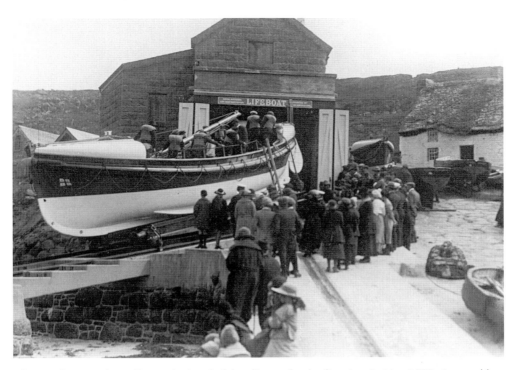

The Newbons on the trolley at the head of the slipway for the first time in May 1922. A crowd has gathered to watch the boat being taken into the boathouse, while the former lifeboat *Ann Newbon* lies alone at the side of the house. (From an old print supplied by Tim Stevens)

was launched for a demonstration of her capabilities in front of the gathered crowd. During her time on station *The Newbons* is credited with saving thirty-six lives and launching on service fifty-four times. The following descriptions cover all of the effective services performed during the twenty-six years she served at Sennen Cove.

The first services performed by the new motor lifeboat took place in 1923. On 29 September 1923, the steamer *Gutfeld*, of Hamburg, ran aground near Cape Cornwall in thick fog when bound from London for Cardiff. *The Newbons* was launched and arrived on the scene at about 6.15 a.m. The Coxswain was asked to board the steamer and, under his direction, the vessel was taken clear of the reef. She then proceeded to Falmouth for repairs and the lifeboat returned to Sennen.

The second service of the year took place on 8 October and proved to be a particularly arduous one. The steamship *City of Westminster*, of Liverpool, bound from Belfast to Rotterdam with seventy-three persons on board, struck the Runnelstone in thick weather. *The Newbons* was launched and arrived on the scene at 11 a.m. when, at the request of the steamer's master, she took off three women and ten of the crew. Transferring these people proved particularly difficult owing to the heavy swell creating a large rise and fall alongside the steamer. The Penlee lifeboat, *The Brothers* (ON.671), then arrived and took on board a number of the crew who had taken to the ship's boats. Then *The Brothers* went alongside the steamer to take off the officers as the steamer was, by this time, rocking heavily in the ground swell. In

Launch of *The Newbons* from the trolley on rails. The boat is dressed overall and the occasion may have been her formal naming ceremony on 29 August 1924. (By courtesy of Bryan Roberts)

total, the Penlee lifeboat saved thirty-five persons from the steamer while the remaining twenty-five were towed to Penzance in their own boats by the local steam drifter *Pioneer*. During the night the steamer's siren was sounding and so both Sennen and Penlee lifeboats had to be launched again, reaching the casualty to find the operating lanyards had been fouled in the rigging causing the siren to sound. The steamer later became a total wreck and extra awards were made to the lifeboatmen for what had been an arduous service.

During 1926, *The Newbons* was called upon twice in the space of a month. On 20 March, she launched to the schooner *Ada*, of Barrow, bound from Barry to Truro with a cargo of coal, which was in difficulties near Cape Cornwall in an easterly wind and rough ground seas. The lifeboat launched to the schooner in response to signals of distress and found the casualty had struck rocks but refloated on the tide. She was in a dangerous position and so one of the lifeboat's crew went on board her to pilot her away from the rocks and, with her crew of six, she eventually got to safety.

The second launch took place on 20 April. *The Newbons* put to sea at 8.15 a.m. in a north-westerly gale and very heavy seas to go to a large steamer reported by the Coastguard to be in need of help two miles west-south-west of Pendeen. The steamer, *Deansway*, of Cardiff, was disabled after her engine had broken down. At first her Captain declined the lifeboat's help but, when another steamship arrived, the lifeboat was asked to pass over a warp. The warp parted and the steamer, with the lifeboat standing by, drifted towards the shore. At this point the lifeboat's engine stopped and would not restart so the crew set sail for St Ives as the steamer, *British Marshal*, had by this time arrived on the scene. Although attempts by the second steamer to pull *Deansway* clear also failed, the *Deansway*'s engines were eventually repaired and she carried on her voyage under her own power.

During the rebuilding of the station described above *The Newbons* was temporarily away from station as she could not be operated during the reconstruction work. She was sent to J.S. White's boatyard in Cowes, where she remained from 22 June 1928 until 25 July 1929 undergoing a complete overhaul and then being stored prior to the completion of the new boathouse. In the absence of the lifeboat, a service was carried out by the motor fishing boat *Tom Sayers* on 30 June 1929. At about 4 p.m.

the Coxswain, Thomas Pender, saw the steamship *Ixia*, of North Shields, bound from Swansea for Constantinople, with coal, in difficulties at Cape Cornwall. In a moderate north-easterly breeze, Pender, with the motor mechanic and four others, put off in the fishing boat and found the steamship ashore. The crew had taken to the ship's boats, but ten men were taken on board the fishing vessel and the other twenty-one were assisted ashore in the boats as the steamer became a total wreck.

The new slipway and boathouse were completed in 1929 and the first launches 'in anger' from the new slipway took place during the summer of 1930 neither of which, however, resulted in a service being affected. On 23 June, *The Newbons* was launched after reports that two men were in difficulty off the Land's End Hotel. She reached the reported position in twenty minutes but the bather and his brother, who was attempting a rescue, had disappeared. On 2 July, the lifeboat was called to the same vicinity as a man had fallen over the cliff, but when the lifeboat arrived nothing was found. In its report of these two launches *The Lifeboat* described them as 'unusual'.

Just over a year later, on 29 August 1931, *The Newbons* was launched after the Coastguard had been alerted to a small boat in difficulties at St Just. The boat, which belonged to Priests Cove, and its three occupants had been caught in a moderate easterly gale and rough sea. Once on the scene, the lifeboat found the men on one of the Brisons Rocks, which would have been covered by the tide. The lifeboat took them on board and towed the small boat, which had a broken boom and damaged sail, to safety.

No effective services were performed by *The Newbons* for almost three years until, during the night of 14-15 July 1934, she was launched to the fishing ketch *Replete*, of Brixham, which was trawling off the Wolf Rock lighthouse. A fire had broken out

The Newbons on the trolley at the head of the slipway for lifeboat day. On the left is the St Just Silver Band, in attendance for the occasion. (By courtesy of Bryan Roberts)

on board the fishing boat and, as the four men on board could not extinguish it, they took to their small boat. It had started at the back of the boiler used for working the trawl–winch, and had spread so quickly that the men were unable to save their personal belongings. The flames were seen from the shore and the lifeboat put out at 12.15 a.m. to find *Replete* ablaze from stem to stern and her crew on board another Brixham vessel, the smack *Radiance*, which had been fishing nearby. They were transferred to the lifeboat which stood by until the burning fishing vessel sank at 4.30 a.m.

During 1936, *The Newbons* was called upon twice. On 10 February she launched after the ketch *Albatros*, of Brest, carrying a cargo of coal from Cardiff for Audierne, hoisted a distress signal during the afternoon when weather–bound in Whitesand Bay. The lifeboat put out at 4 p.m. into a rough sea and heavy rain and found the ketch's crew of four, together with their dog, in the ship's boat. They were taken on board the lifeboat, with some difficulty, and landed at Sennen.

On 21 December, *The Newbons* assisted and stood by the steamship *Mina*, of Parnu. The steamer had broken her rudder shaft in a strong south-westerly breeze and rough sea and the Isles of Scilly packet boat *Scillonian* was on hand while Sennen and Penlee lifeboats were called. The Sennen boat launched at 11.50 a.m. and found the steamer about eight miles south-west of the Tol Pedn lookout. She assisted as *Scillonian* towed the casualty and later also joined up to assist towing the vessel. In the bad weather the two ropes parted but temporary repairs were made as *Mina* was not in immediate danger. The lifeboat stood by until no longer needed and then, as the weather was too rough to rehouse at Sennen, made for Penzance harbour where she stayed overnight. *Scillonian* reported that she was alongside the casualty about a mile from the Wolf Rock, with the vessel requesting a tow to Falmouth. Tugs later arrived to assist the steamer to port.

This fine photograph of *The Newbons* being recovered shows clearly the deck layout of the 40ft motor self-righting design. The engine casing can be seen just in front of the small shelter, with end boxes at bow and stern to provide the righting capability. Apart from the shelter, the boat was essentially open, similar to her man-powered predecessors, and offered the crew little or no protection. (By courtesy of the RNLI)

The Newbons approaching the lifeboat house returning from exercise on 28 August 1936. This photograph shows the house after the alterations which saw the railway lines and trolley removed and a slipway launch procedure introduced. The house was enlarged considerably to accommodate a turntable inside. Shore helpers are making ready for the lifeboat's return. (From an old postcard supplied by a Shoreline member)

Rehousing the lifeboat at Sennen in bad weather was often very difficult and, even after what turned out to be relatively routine services, she sometimes had to seek shelter at Penzance before getting back to her station when the weather had moderated. One such occasion was on the afternoon of 16 February 1937 after Coxswain Thomas Pender received a message from the Coastguard that a steamer had broken down due to mechanical problems about a mile north of the Longships and needed assistance. *The Newbons* was launched at 4.20 p.m. into a strong north-westerly gale and very rough sea. She reached the steamer, *Svanhild*, of Elsinore, twenty-five minutes later and found her at anchor with another small steamer standing by. The lifeboat also stood by until the *Svanhild's* engines had been repaired and the vessel was on its way. Because conditions were too bad to rehouse the lifeboat, she made for Penzance where she spent the night but it was not until 18 February that she returned to station.

On 18 December 1938, the schooner *Bretonne*, of Treguier, with a cargo of coal bound for Brest from Cardiff, sheltered in Whitesand Bay from a south-easterly gale. At 7.35 p.m. she started burning distress flares and, as soon as these were sighted, *The Newbons* was launched, getting clear of the slipway at 8.05 p.m. The lifeboat found the schooner had parted one cable, was dragging the other and was leaking very badly. A heaving line was thrown to the schooner and, with some difficulty, the lifeboatmen succeeded in getting the schooner's crew of five on board. The lifeboat then returned to her station, where she arrived at 9.45 p.m. However, as it was low tide, the boat could not be rehoused until 11.30 p.m. so the crew and launchers had to wait on what was a bitterly cold night. The schooner was presumed to have sunk during the night.

The Newbons returning to station from exercise on 28 August 1936, with lines attached bow and stern ready for the recovery. (By courtesy of the RNLI)

When the Second World War broke out in 1939, its impact on the lifeboat service's operations was considerable. The removal of navigation and coastal lights, so vital when negotiating Land's End, and the loss of younger crew members were just two of the many difficulties that had to be surmounted. The danger of enemy aircraft and mines were other hazards, while many of the services performed by *The Newbons* involved searching for missing aircraft that were often not found. Her first launch of the war took place on 18 September 1939 after an aeroplane had been reported down in the sea. However, soon after launching, she was recalled by the Coastguard. On 25 November 1940 she was asked to search for survivors after a naval and air battle ten miles off the Wolf Rock lighthouse. Penlee and Lizard lifeboats were also involved but nothing was found apart from a large patch of oil.

Another fruitless launch was undertaken on 2 February 1941 after the Coastguard had reported a vessel in distress in a strong north-easterly gale and very rough sea. *The Newbons* was launched at 6 p.m. to investigate and found the steamship *Heire*, of Oslo, about three miles north-west of the Brisons having lost her propeller. She was waiting for a tug and did not need the lifeboat's help, so the lifeboat returned to station where the crew remained on standby. Three hours later the casualty fired a red rocket and was thought to be ashore on the Shark's Fin. However, as the weather had got worse, it was not possible to launch the lifeboat again. Penlee lifeboat *W.&S.* (ON.736) launched at midnight and found the steamer in a very dangerous position still waiting for the tug so she stood by until, nine hours later, the tug arrived and began towing the steamer to safety.

The Sennen lifeboatmen undertook several more services during 1941 but none resulted in a positive outcome. One such service took place on 14 April 1941 when red flares were reported off Cape Cornwall but when *The Newbons* arrived on the scene nothing could be found. It later transpired that the flares were Holmes lights from lifebuoys of the Belgian steamer *Arbel*, of Antwerp, which had been blown off her when she was bombed and then sunk. The seventeen survivors out of her crew of twenty came ashore at St Ives.

On 27 May 1941, at about 10.45 p.m., the auxiliary cruiser *Registan* was bombed by four enemy aeroplanes and caught fire six miles north-west of Sennen Cove. As the lifeboat was being overhauled, the Second Coxswain, Edward Nicholas, and four men put out in the fishing boat *Ruby* at 11 p.m. They succeeded in saving four men, one of whom was badly injured, from a raft close to the burning steamer. Then, as they attempted to use a Morse signal lamp, an enemy aeroplane flew over, having been attracted by the light, and machine gunned the boat but fortunately no damage was done. The rescued men were landed at Sennen at 3.15 a.m. with rescued and rescuers grateful at having escaped alive.

The next three services performed by *The Newbons* all involved crashed aircraft. On 21 August 1941 an aeroplane was reported down in the sea off Cape Cornwall but nothing was found. The same occurred on 6 September 1941, with a missing aircaft of which no trace was discovered. Just over a year later, on 12 September 1942, the Coastguard reported an aeroplane crashed about four miles north-west of Cape Cornwall. At 10.45 p.m. *The Newbons* was launched into the calm sea but all she found were pieces of aeroplane and burning oil. After a search of the area, she returned to her station at 12.45 a.m. the following day. On 8 October 1942, she again launched to an aeroplane reported to have crashed into the sea 200 yards off Pendeen lighthouse in a strong squally north-west wind and rough sea. At 2.34 p.m. the lifeboat put off and a Lysander aircraft guided her to where the two airmen in 'Mae West' jackets were floating unconscious. The lifeboatmen took them on board *The Newbons* but their efforts at resuscitation failed and, although she returned to Sennen at 5 p.m., the bodies could not be landed for over an hour due to the state of the tide.

The Newbons continued to put out to reports of crashed aircraft. On 24 December, a Whitley bomber crashed and four men from it were rescued by a patrol trawler while the rest drowned. On 1 May 1943, a Spitfire was reported down but, despite searching, the lifeboatmen found nothing. On 27 June 1944 *The Newbons* searched in vain for a small fishing boat with two men on board which had been reported missing. Three days later, it was back to war casualties after a report had been received from the Longships lighthouse at 8.18 p.m. that a boat was adrift about half a mile

Launch of *The Newbons* down the long slipway after the railway lines and trolley had been replaced. The remains of the rail tracks can just be made out at the far left. (From an old postcard supplied by David Gooch)

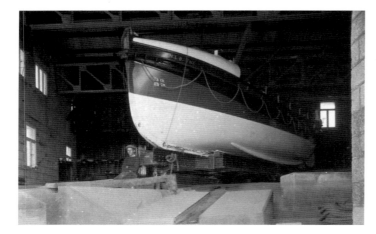

Left: The Newbons inside the lifeboat house on the turntable pointed towards the long slipway. (By courtesy of the RNLI)

Below: Launch of *The Newbons* down the long slipway. This photograph gives a good impression of the length of the slipway and the rocky beach over which launching takes place. (By courtesy of the RNLI)

north-west of the Longships, representing a danger to other vessels in the area. *The Newbons* was launched into a squally north-west wind and found the US Army's motor launch MT.392 near the Brisons. It had apparently been abandoned in a hurry with its crew's personal effects still on board and so was towed back to Sennen.

During the first three months of 1945, as the war was coming to an end, *The Newbons* undertook four services. On 21 January 1945, the lifeboat was launched at 3.30 p.m. after the naval authorities requested her assistance, via the Coastguard, with regard to a vessel four miles south-by-west of the Longships. Just over an hour after launching the lifeboat found the Liberty steamer *George Hawley*, of Savannah, Georgia, USA, which was in difficulties after being torpedoed. All her crew except five had been saved and, as everything was covered with oil, the remaining five got into one of their own boats which was towed by the lifeboat to a tug, which itself was ready to tow the steamer to safety. Only two lives had been lost in the incident and the steamer was successfully taken to Falmouth while the lifeboat returned to her station at 7.45 p.m.

On 24 February 1945 *The Newbons* was launched after an unknown vessel had been torpedoed, but the lifeboatmen only found wreckage. Just over a month later, on

22 March, *The Newbons* put out to the steamship *Empire Kingsley*, of Greenock. The steamer had been torpedoed at 3.40 p.m., seven miles north-west of the lifeboat station. The explosion had been heard at Sennen and within ten minutes the lifeboat was at sea. She reached the scene where she was called alongside an escort vessel on board which were forty-nine of the crew of the torpedoed steamship. They were all transferred to the lifeboat, including four on stretchers, and landed at Sennen at 6 p.m.

The final service of the war took place on 29 March 1945. At 7.33 a.m. a message was received that a vessel, four miles north-north-west of Pen-men-dhu, needed help. In just over ten minutes *The Newbons* put to sea in a strong wind and rough sea and, at 8.25 a.m., found the frigate HMCS *Teme* (K.458), of the Royal Canadian Navy, which had her stern nearly blown off by a torpedo. The lifeboat was taken alongside and asked to search in the wake of the corvette for two missing men. She found one and returned to stand by until another vessel arrived on the scene to take the corvette in tow. After escorting the vessels until a large tug arrived, by when the Penlee lifeboat *W. & S.* also on hand, *The Newbons* returned to station. The Penlee lifeboat ended up taking fifty-seven men off the frigate after both the tow between it and the corvette parted and the new tow between the naval vessel and the tug had also failed.

After the war had ended, *The Newbons* only performed two further service launches, neither of which resulted in a positive outcome, before being replaced at the station. On 26 February 1946, a steamer taking in water called for help but managed to get the leak under control before the lifeboat had launched. On 3 February 1948, the lifeboat launched at about 2 p.m. to the motor vessel *Java*, of Rotterdam, which was bound for Swansea and was showing signals of distress three miles north-north-west of Cape Cornwall. In overcast conditions with a rough sea the lifeboat put out but was recalled after the Coastguard reported the vessel heading towards St Ives under her own power. This proved to be the final launch of *The Newbons* – within six months she had been replaced at the station by a new and more powerful lifeboat.

High water launch of *The Newbons* down the long slipway. The building that can be seen immediately to the left of and behind the boathouse is the lifeboat house of 1875. (From an old photograph supplied by David Gooch)

After leaving Sennen, she was reallocated to Port St Mary, on the Isle of Man, where she served for a year during which time she launched once on service. After this, in March 1951, she was sold out of service by the RNLI into private ownership and was converted into the yacht *Fair Lady*. She was based for a time on the North Wales coast and was at Birkenhead in 1974 but her subsequent whereabouts are not known.

The crew of *The Newbons,* wearing kapok life-jackets which were introduced in 1904, in front of their boat at the head of the long slipway. This photograph probably dates from the 1930s as the railway launching system has been abolished. From left to right: Jack Roberts, Tom Vale George, Edward George, Cecil Roberts, Edward Nicholas, Tom Pender, Nathanial George, Edmund George, Henry Nicholas. (By courtesy of Bryan Roberts)

Sennen Cove lifeboatmen with *The Newbons* in a photograph probably taken during the 1930s. From left to right, back row: James Mathie George, Harry James, Edward George, Henry Nicholas, -?-, Nathaniel George. Front row: Tom Vale George, Edmund George, Edward Nicholas. (From an old postcard by courtesy of Bryan Roberts)

4

The post-war era

Susan Ashley

41ft Watson motor lifeboat *Susan Ashley* on trials in 1948 prior to coming to Sennen. (By courtesy of RNLI Sennen Cove)

The arrival, in July 1948, of *Susan Ashley,* a 41ft Watson motor lifeboat, opened a new chapter in the history of the Sennen Cove station. She was the station's first lifeboat to be fitted with a cabin: the aluminium alloy superstructure was, in effect, a small shelter over the engine room and provided the crew a little protection from the worst of the elements as well as offering a forward cabin for survivors. She was also fitted with a wireless and loud hailer and was regarded as a significant advance over her predecessor. Provided from the legacy of Charles Carr Ashley, who died at

Mentone in France in 1906, she was named after the donor's mother, the third lifeboat in the RNLI fleet to be so named; the first served at Lyme Regis from 1891 to 1915 and the second at Brooke, on the Isle of Wight, from 1907 to 1937.

Powered by two Weyburn AE6 six-cylinder petrol engines, each of 35bhp, developing 3,300 rpm, the new lifeboat reached a maximum speed of 7.82 knots consuming almost seven gallons of fuel per hour during trials and, at this speed, had a radius of action of sixty-three nautical miles. Her cruising speed was seven knots, at which rate the radius of action increased to eighty-nine nautical miles. She carried a total of 112 gallons of fuel. As post-war marine technology advanced, small marine diesels were developed and gradually introduced into the lifeboat service and many existing lifeboats were re-engined. *Susan Ashley* was fitted with new twin 47hp Parsons Porbeagle diesels in 1963, which increased her range while also reducing the risk of fire on board. During the quarter of a century that she served at Sennen Cove, *Susan Ashley* is credited with saving sixty-four lives and launching eighty-seven times on service; the majority of her launches are described in this section.

The naming ceremony for the new lifeboat was arranged for 4 September 1948. However, just before 8 a.m. the previous day, *Susan Ashley* was called into action for the first time. She launched in a north-westerly gale just after 8 a.m. to go to the help of a trawler which had trouble with its engines. The lifeboatmen searched a

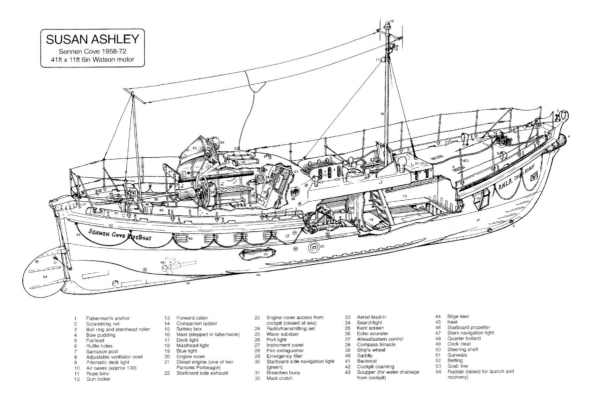

SUSAN ASHLEY
Sennen Cove 1958-72
41ft x 11ft 6in Watson motor

1	Fisherman's anchor	13	Forward cabin	23	Engine room access from	33	Aerial lead-in	44	Bilge keel
2	Scrambling net	14	Companion ladder		cockpit (closed at sea)	34	Searchlight	45	Keel
3	Bull ring and stemhead roller	15	Battery box	24	Radio/transmitting set	35	Kent screen	46	Starboard propeller
4	Bow pudding	16	Mast (stepped in tabernacle)	25	Wave subduer	36	Echo sounder	47	Stern navigation light
5	Fairlead	17	Deck light	26	Port light	37	Ahead/astern control	48	Quarter bollard
6	Ruffle holes	18	Masthead light	27	Instrument panel	38	Compass binacle	49	Deck cleat
7	Sampson post	19	Blue light	28	Fire extinguisher	39	Ship's wheel	50	Steering shaft
8	Adjustable ventilator cowl	20	Engine room	29	Emergency tiller	40	Saddfly	51	Gunwale
9	Prismatic deck light	21	Diesel engine (one of two	30	Starboard side navigation light	41	Backrest	52	Belting
10	Air cases (approx 130)		Parsons Porbeagle)		(green)	42	Cockpit coaming	53	Grab line
11	Rope bins	22	Starboard side exhaust	31	Breeches buoy	43	Scupper (for water drainage	54	Rudder (raised for launch and
12	Gun locker			32	Mast crutch		from cockpit)		recovery)

Cutaway drawing showing the 41ft Watson motor lifeboat *Susan Ashley*.

First launch of *Susan Ashley* after she arrived on station in July 1948. In the foreground on the left can clearly be seen the remains of the railway tracks used for launching until 1929. (From an old postcard supplied by David Gooch)

wide area but could not find the trawler which, it was discovered afterwards, had repaired her engine and continued on her way. Because the weather was too bad for rehousing at Sennen, *Susan Ashley* made for Newlyn where she stayed until 5 September. As a result, she was not present for the ceremony which, perhaps unusually, still went ahead as planned, except for the actual christening itself. During the ceremony, speeches were made by Mr J.T. Nicholas, Chairman of the Branch, Captain G.R. Cousins, DSC, RN, the District Inspector, and several other notable persons. The Assistant Bishop of Truro, the Right Revd John Holden said prayers while hymns were sung accompanied by the St Ives Town Band. The formal christening took place on 2 October when the lifeboat was named by Lady Burnett after she had been dedicated by Revd W.R. Morris, Rector of Sennen.

Susan Ashley performed her first effective service just over a week after her full naming, on 11 October 1948. At 4.35 a.m. the Coastguard passed on a message from the steamship *Woodlark,* bound for Barry from Dieppe, that she had been in collision with and sunk the fishing vessel *Saphir,* of Camaret, three miles northwest of the Longships. She had picked up one survivor of the fishing vessel's crew of six. Because of the state of the tide, the lifeboat could not get away until 5.39 a.m. when she launched into a light breeze and slight swell. She found the steamer eight miles north west of the Longships and helped to search for the missing men but found nothing except an upturned dinghy and some wreckage. At the request of the steamer, the lifeboat transferred the survivor from the steamer to another French fishing boat, *Corindon,* also of Camaret, and then returned to station, arriving at Sennen at 11 a.m.

Just over a fortnight later, on 26 October 1948, *Susan Ashley* was called into action again. Her assistance was requested at 8.15 a.m. after the Coastguard had received a message from the tug *Superman*, of Hull. The tug, together with another tug, *Airman,*

Left: Susan Ashley is launched at the end of her naming ceremony on 2 October 1948 watched by a crowd of well-wishers and supporters. (By courtesy of the RNLI)

Below: Susan Ashley is prepared for recovery, with heaving lines attached bow and stern as she approaches the short slipway. This photograph shows the fine lines of the 41ft Watson motor lifeboat which served at Sennen with distinction for twenty-five years. (From an old postcard supplied by David Gooch)

had been towing the forepart of the steamer *Empire Flamingo* from Arromanches to Newport for breaking up when it began to sink three miles south of the Longships. The lifeboat launched at 8.33 a.m. into a moderate northerly breeze with heavy ground swell. She found the hulk and rescued the four men on it, landing them safely at Newlyn. As the lifeboat reached port, a wireless message was received saying that the forepart had foundered. *Empire Flamingo* was classed as a Special Service Vessel and sunk as a blockship in February 1944 on one of the Normandy beaches. She had originally been the American cargo liner *Jolee* of 5,200 tons.

As Sennen Cove is the mainland lifeboat station closest to the Isles of Scilly, on occasions the lifeboat has been called to assist with an incident there. At 9.22 a.m. on 6 January 1952 the medical officer on the Isles of Scilly telephoned to say that a patient at St Mary's needed an immediate operation and, owing to thick fog, the surgeon and his staff could not fly over from the mainland. So, at 11.20 p.m., *Susan Ashley* was launched with three doctors and a sister from the West Cornwall Hospital in Penzance. The lifeboat took them to St Mary's in a slight swell, a light westerly breeze and through patches of fog. The doctors were able to save the patient's life and, just over nine hours after launching, *Susan Ashley* returned to station.

The other service of 1952 took place on 20 July when *Susan Ashley* went to assist the 17-ton auxiliary sailing yacht *Morena*, of London, which was on passage from Dartmouth for Falmouth with a crew of three when she lost her way at night. The lifeboat launched at 7.30 a.m. and found the yacht three-quarters of a mile north of the Longships. *Susan Ashley* towed her well clear of the Longships Reef and into

Susan Ashley on the turntable inside the lifeboat house. This picture is a still from the film *Bequest to a village*. (By courtesy of the RNLI)

Mount's Bay when, with a favourable wind, the yacht was able to continue on her own and the lifeboat returned to station.

Susan Ashley performed another service to a yacht on 18 April 1953 after the keeper of the Pendeen lighthouse telephoned the Coxswain to say he had seen the vessel in distress off the Three Stone Oar Rocks. The lifeboat launched at 5.30 p.m. and found the Bermuda-rigged yacht *Larry*, of Southampton, with a crew of three, two miles west of the lighthouse. She had lost her mainsail in a choppy sea and the auxiliary engine had broken down while she was bound for Highbridge. The lifeboat towed her to Newlyn, then returned to Sennen at 11.35 p.m.

More than three years elapsed before *Susan Ashley's* services were needed again. On 30 July 1956, at 8.18 p.m., the St Just Coastguard reported that a yacht had been seen off the Longships circling but with the engine running. *Susan Ashley* was launched at 8.35 p.m. in a moderate sea and gentle breeze to investigate. She reached the yacht *Westo II* a mile and a half north-west of the Longships and the lifeboatmen found her abandoned but with her diesel engine still functioning. One of the lifeboat crew went on board, attached a tow rope and the yacht was towed to Newlyn arriving at 11.15 p.m. The lifeboat stayed overnight in Newlyn harbour and did not return to her station until 9.40 a.m. the following day. It was later discovered that the yacht's crew of three had been taken off by the motor vessel *Corncrake* on 29 July when the yacht was off Land's End.

Almost five more years passed before *Susan Ashley* was called upon again to perform a service, and then it only involved standing by a vessel. On 28 June 1961, the Coastguard informed the honorary secretary that the Southern Rescue Coordination Centre in Plymouth had asked if the lifeboat could put to sea and stand by while a helicopter flew a doctor to the French trawler *Enfant Des Houl*, which was south-south-east of the Isles of Scilly and on board which was a sick man. The lifeboat launched at 8.28 p.m. and stood by while the helicopter accomplished its mission then returned to Sennen at 12.15 a.m. on 29 June. The St Mary's (Isle of Scilly) lifeboat went out to the trawler and circled while the sick man was taken off, afterwards putting the doctor on board the trawler which returned to Newlyn.

During the summer of 1962, *Susan Ashley* was called upon to perform a number of services, many routine in nature, but the first of which had an unhappy conclusion. On 9 May, she was launched just after 7.30 p.m. when it was reported that a man was trapped on the cliffs at Land's End. Once on scene, the lifeboatmen saw that one of the Coastguards had been lowered from the cliff top to a man who was lying on a ledge. The Coastguard asked the lifeboat to fetch a punt as the man was too badly injured to be hoisted up the cliff. So the lifeboat returned to Sennen Cove, obtained a punt with three men to man it and returned to the cliffs. With some difficulty the punt was taken in to the cliffs but the man had died of his injuries before he could be helped. The body was lowered 30ft into the punt which was then towed back to Sennen.

On 9 July 1962, *Susan Ashley* put out at 8.25 a.m. to the cabin cruiser *Eldora*, which had broken down two miles north of Cape Cornwall after running out of fuel. The lifeboat towed the cruiser to Newlyn and was back at Sennen at 3.10 p.m. Just over two weeks later, on 28 July, she put out at 5 p.m. to assist two men who had got into difficulties swimming from Land's End to the rock Armed Knight. The

Susan Ashley tows a yacht into Newlyn Harbour. (Bryan Roberts, by courtesy of RNLI Sennen Cove)

swimmers were taken off the rock and landed at Sennen Cove at 5.30 p.m. On 4 August, the motor tug *Sally*, of Rochester, which had two crew on board and was bound for Swansea, broke down four miles off the Longships Lighthouse. At 9.45 a.m. the lifeboat launched and, at the master's request, towed the tug to Newlyn. The final service of the summer took place on 25 August after the Coastguard had informed the honorary secretary that a young woman had been swept from rocks at Land's End by a large wave. *Susan Ashley* put out at 1.27 p.m. in a choppy sea with heavy ground swell and was directed by people on the cliff top to where the woman was floating. She was faced downwards, about 200 yards out close to Enys Dodman and, when picked up, she was found not to be alive.

Soon after this service, *Susan Ashley* went away for a routine overhaul and, in her place, came reserve lifeboat *Edmund and Mary Robinson* (ON.812), which had been built in 1938 and served as the New Brighton No.2 lifeboat until 1950. While at Sennen, the reserve lifeboat was involved in only one service which proved to be a particularly difficult one. At 5.21 a.m. on 3 November 1962 the Coastguard informed the Coxswain that a vessel was ashore on rocks off Land's End. The lifeboat was launched into a very rough sea and moderate south-westerly breeze and, at 6.20 a.m., found the 25-ton trawler *Jeanne Gougy*, of Dieppe, about 100m to the north east of Land's End point in the high-sided vertical-faced cove Tali Sound. The trawler had left Dieppe for the fishing grounds off the south of Ireland and was due back at her home port on 4 November. However, she got into difficulty off Sennen and ended up ashore at Land's End. Once on the scene, the lifeboat fired a parachute flare which lit up the area and showed the trawler lying on her side on the rocks at the foot of the cliffs where, in the aftermath of a storm, an exceptionally heavy ground swell made conditions particularly difficult. The lifeboat could not get any closer than a hundred yards. A life-saving apparatus team on the cliff top fired several lines over the wreck but the trawler's crew could not secure them as their vessel was completely submerged by the swell. Minutes after the sixth rocket had been fired across, the trawler crashed over onto her port side and several men were washed out of the wheelhouse. By dawn she was on her side in a tangle of masts and ropes.

At 8.15 a.m. a helicopter from RAF Chivenor arrived and both helicopter and lifeboat then carried out a search for the crew of the trawler. The lifeboat found two of the crew, but sadly neither was alive. The helicopter also picked up a body then, at 9 a.m., left for Penzance to land the body and refuel. As it seemed clear that nobody else was left alive on the trawler, the lifeboat also left to land the bodies. *Edmund and Mary Robinson* had to make for Newlyn as it was impossible to recover at Sennen but, at 11.30 a.m., people on the cliffs saw signs of life on the trawler and so the helicopter was recalled. Penlee lifeboat *Solomon Browne* (ON.954) was also launched and arrived on the scene at 2 p.m., by which time four survivors had been rescued by the LSA and two injured men lifted off by helicopter in two separate operations. As soon as the Sennen crew were told of the situation they returned to Newlyn and put out again, arriving at 3.45 p.m. Both lifeboats and the helicopter searched the area further but found nothing else.

It was later learned that the trawler had a crew of eighteen, twelve of whom lost their lives. No explanations could be found as to why the trawler had been wrecked. She had left Waterford the previous evening and the weather had been rough all the way across, but she was built to withstand much worse conditions. As a result of this rescue and in recognition of their efforts, Coxswain Henry Nicholas, Second Coxswain J.H. Nicholas, Bowman E. George and Mechanic R. George were awarded the French Maritime Medal in Bronze. Sergeant E.C. Smith, of the RAF, who was lowered down to the wrecked trawler to save the two injured men, was awarded the George Medal and also the silver medal of the Société Nationale des Hospitaliers Sauveteurs Bretons. The wreck of the trawler was subsequently bought by a scrap merchant who managed to salvage some items from it, including the ship's bell, its radio and chronometer.

In 1963 *Susan Ashley* returned to station and performed one service during the year. At 12.06 p.m. on 13 September the St Just Coastguard reported a vessel aground at Portheras Cove. After further inspection, the Coastguard requested that the lifeboat launch and so, in thick fog with visibility down to only ten yards, *Susan Ashley* put out at 1.40 p.m. under the command of the Second Coxswain. Forty minutes later she arrived at the casualty, the cargo vessel *Alacrity*, which was carrying coal, with a crew of eight, bound from Swansea to Belgium. Two lifeboatmen went on board and helped to launch the ship's boat, which was then used to bring a salvage punt from the shore. At 3.30 p.m. the lifeboat anchored astern of the casualty to await further developments and remained standing by until just after 7 p.m. when she was released from her duties, and returned to station.

The next service performed by *Susan Ashley* proved to be a particularly notable one. At 4.03 a.m. on 24 March 1964 the honorary secretary Captain H.B. Harvey was informed by the St Just Coastguard that a Belgian trawler was ashore at Land's End. At 4.30 a.m. *Susan Ashley* was launched into a south-westerly wind and poor visibility due to a combination of fog and rain. Five minutes after launching,

Wreck of the trawler *Jeanne Gougy*, of Dieppe, on the north side of Land's End point, November 1962. (By courtesy of RNLI Sennen Cove)

Relief 41ft Watson motor *Edmund and Mary Robinson* returns from attending the trawler *Jeanne Gougy*, November 1962. (Ken Young)

Coxswain Henry Nicholas saw the 90-ton trawler, *Victoire Roger*, of Ostend, on fire and ashore in Gamper Cove, a steep rocky inlet near Land's End. The lifeboat arrived on the scene fifteen minutes after launching.

Coxswain Nicholas' first intention had been to stand off and use the rocket apparatus and breaches buoy but, as he approached the trawler, he could see the vessel's crew standing on the poop in the light of the flames and in immediate and considerable danger. He therefore decided to go alongside straight away and take them off. The lifeboat crew were stationed forward on board their boat as Coxswain

The cargo vessel *Alacrity* stranded at Portheras Cove, September 1963. (Derek Harvey, by courtesy of Tim Stevens)

Nicholas skilfully manoeuvred her alongside the starboard quarter of the trawler. This exercise was partially successful as four men were taken off. Unfortunately, though, a heavy sea then drove the lifeboat into the cove where she touched bottom. By skilful use of the engines, Coxswain Nicholas brought the lifeboat astern and safely out of the cove, although another heavy sea broke over her stern. The lifeboat crew then learned that the skipper, who had a broken arm, was still on board the casualty so the lifeboat was immediately taken alongside again. In spite of his injuries, the skipper was successfully taken off and, within a few minutes, the whole rescue operation had been completed. Coxswain Nicholas then made for Newlyn where a doctor and an ambulance were both standing by. The lifeboat reached Newlyn harbour at 6.16 a.m. and safely landed the survivors. She returned to her station at 11.35 a.m. and was rehoused half an hour later.

As a result of this service, the Bronze second service clasp was awarded to the sixty-two-year-old Coxswain Nicholas who, nearly forty-five years earlier, had won his first Bronze medal at the age of seventeen when *Ann Newbon* had saved four men from the rocks after a motor launch had been driven ashore onto the Longships on 30 November 1919. Medal Service Certificates were issued to the other members of the crew involved in this rescue: Second Coxswain Eric Pengilly, Bowman Edmund George, Mechanic Richard George, Assistant Mechanic Maurice Hutchens, crew members Kenneth G. Bowden, Cecil H. Botterell and Hedley Hutchings.

The next calls on the Sennen lifeboat were somewhat more routine-like in nature. At 10.30 a.m. on 1 July 1965 the motor boat *Wheal Geevor* was reported to have struck a rock three-quarters of a mile west of Cape Cornwall and her crew of seven were bailing. *Susan Ashley* launched at 10.40 a.m., three hours after high water, in a light north-easterly breeze and slight sea. At the request of the motor boat's skipper, the lifeboat escorted *Wheal Geevor* to Newlyn and then returned to her station.

At 4.33 p.m. on 25 September 1965, the honorary secretary was notified that the fishing boat *Spray* with two skin divers on board was in difficulties off Porthchapel beach. *Susan Ashley* launched twelve minutes after the honorary secretary had been alerted and towed the fishing boat to Newlyn harbour, then returned to her station where she arrived at 7.20 p.m.

On occasions the lifeboat has been called upon to assist in a medical emergency at sea: one such incident took place in March 1966. At 11.20 a.m. on 30 March the port medical officer at Penzance informed the honorary secretary that the motor vessel *Hille Oldendorff*, of Lübeck, which was about nine miles north west of the Longships lighthouse, needed medical help for an injured seaman. At 11.45 a.m. *Susan Ashley* was launched with a doctor on board. The lifeboat reached the motor vessel, which was seven miles north-west of the lifeboat station, and transferred the doctor on board. The injured man, who had a suspected fracture of the skull, was soon transferred to the lifeboat which then returned to her station at 1.45 p.m., where an ambulance was waiting.

During July 1966, the services of *Susan Ashley* were required twice in the space of just nine days. On 21 July 1966, two men were reported to be cut off by the tide in a cave near Land's End. A dinghy was put aboard *Susan Ashley* and she launched at

Sennen Cove lifeboat crew from the late 1960s. From left to right: Bill Pender, Derek Chappell, Maurice Hutchens, Coxswain Eric Pengilly, Cyril Botterel, Philip Shannon, Eric Ellis. (By courtesy of RNLI Sennen Cove)

5.55 p.m. in a moderate to fresh north-easterly wind. When she arrived at Land's End, Coastguards burned a flare to indicate the position of the cave. The dinghy was then lowered into the water and two of the lifeboat crew took it to the cliff. The two youths, who were stranded on a ledge, were taken into the dinghy and transferred to the lifeboat.

On 30 July 1966, a motor boat a mile north-north-west of Cape Cornwall fired a distress rocket. At 8.45 p.m., *Susan Ashley* was launched, putting out into a strong north-westerly wind and very rough sea. She proceeded to the motor launch *Kathleen* and took off one of her crew. The lifeboat then escorted the casualty to St Ives Bay, where the St Ives inshore rescue boat (IRB) met them and saw *Kathleen* to a safe anchorage while the lifeboat returned to her station. The IRB took the casualty's crew ashore where a car was waiting to take them to their homes. *Susan Ashley* arrived back at Sennen Cove at 3.30 a.m.

During June 1967, *Susan Ashley* was called out on service twice. On 11 June, she was launched at 10.30 a.m. after reports had been received that a motor cruiser was in difficulties with engine failure near Cape Cornwall. The weather was good and the lifeboat quickly arrived on the scene to find the motor cruiser *Potemkin* with five people on board. The casualty was taken in tow and a course was set for Newlyn where both boats arrived just before 2 p.m. The lifeboat returned to her station where she was rehoused at 5 p.m.

Just over a week later, on 20 June, reports were received that flares had been seen to the north-west of Cape Cornwall. At 4.45 a.m., *Susan Ashley* was launched in a moderate westerly wind and choppy sea. The lifeboat found two people on board the yacht *Tropacara* which had a broken-down engine. One of the lifeboat crew went on board the yacht and it was towed to St Ives. Because it was low water at Sennen, the lifeboat stayed at St Ives until 11.45 a.m. and reached her station at 2.20 p.m.

Susan Ashley undertook another routine service on 28 August 1967 after the Coastguard informed the honorary secretary that a French trawler was in difficulty a mile north of the Wolf Rock lighthouse. It was taking in water and was drifting so the lifeboat launched at 3.56 p.m. in light winds and a slight sea. As the lifeboat approached the trawler the Coxswain saw another French trawler manoeuvring close by and then take the disabled vessel in tow towards Newlyn. The lifeboat escorted both vessels until the lifeboatmen were sure that no further assistance was required. They then returned to station.

In April 1968 *Susan Ashley* was called upon to perform a long service in difficult conditions to an unusual casualty. At noon on 12 April the coastguard informed the honorary secretary that the exhibition galleon *Hispaniola,* at anchor five miles west of Cape Cornwall, was in difficulty with a broken-down engine. With the wind increasing and a flood tide *Susan Ashley* was launched at 2.30 p.m. in a strong east-south-easterly breeze and rough sea three hours after low water. The lifeboat reached *Hispaniola* at 4.20 p.m. to find she was drifting about fifteen miles off Cape Cornwall. *Hispaniola* was taken in tow by the lifeboat but the strong headwinds and adverse tide, together with the high superstructure of the galleon, rendered the tow very difficult. The lifeboatmen continued as best they could and the casualty was brought into St Ives Bay at 12.15 a.m. on 13 April. They dropped anchor in the bay as there was insufficient water to berth in St Ives harbour and the lifeboat stood by throughout

Above right: Henry Nicholas, who served as Coxswain from 1959 until 1967. He was awarded the Bronze medals for services in 1919 and 1964. (By courtesy of RNLI Sennen Cove)

Above left: Coxswain Eric Pengilly took over from Henry Nicholas in 1967 and was Coxswain for more than a decade. (By courtesy of RNLI Sennen Cove)

the night. At 4.45 a.m. *Susan Ashley*, with the assistance of St Ives IRB which had been launched to assist, succeeded in manoeuvring the galleon to a safe berth, an operation which was carried out with great difficulty and involved the closest cooperation between lifeboat and IRB. At 6.30 a.m. *Susan Ashley* left St Ives and the IRB returned to her station an hour later.

During the return passage to Sennen, a request was received at 8 a.m. to take off a keeper from the Wolf Rock lighthouse who was seriously ill and required hospital treatment. The lifeboat reached the lighthouse at 9.10 a.m. but the rough seas made it impossible to take the man off. A helicopter was requested and the lifeboat stood by until the helicopter lifted the sick man from the lantern platform. *Susan Ashley* then returned to her station and was recovered at 4 p.m. having been away for more than twenty-four hours. The owner of *Hispaniola* made a donation to the Institution's funds in appreciation of the Sennen lifeboat's help.

At 3.55 p.m. on 23 August 1968 a report was received that a girl had been washed off the rocks at Land's End and a man had jumped into the sea to help her. *Susan Ashley* launched at 4.07 p.m. in a moderate north-easterly wind and moderate sea to help. On reaching the scene, the lifeboat found three people clinging to a life-buoy. To haul them ashore might have proved fatal, so the lifeboat was brought within 10ft of them and they were thrown a breeches buoy which they reached at the first attempt. They were then quickly hauled aboard the lifeboat and wrapped in blankets as the lifeboat returned to station. At 4.30 p.m. she reached the slipway where the survivors were landed and two were taken to hospital by ambulance.

During 1969, *Susan Ashley* performed a series of routine rescues. At 6.59 p.m. on 16 April it was learnt that a two-masted schooner yacht had broken down about a mile south of Tol Pedn. Although the yacht resumed her passage, she broke down

Susan Ashley on the short slipway during recovery. (Derek Harvey)

again close to the Runnelstone Buoy so at 7.58 p.m. *Susan Ashley* was launched. The lifeboat soon reached the yacht *Mahe*, of Faversham, with a crew of two on board. The casualty was towed to Newlyn, arriving there at 10.45 p.m. but, owing to the state of the tide, the lifeboat remained at Newlyn until 2 a.m. returning to her station at 4.50 a.m. on 17 April.

At 8.22 p.m. on 13 August *Susan Ashley* was launched to a yacht in difficulties a mile and a half from the coastguard look-out. One man, who was found on a malibou board trying to make for the shore, was taken on board the lifeboat. At 9 p.m. the lifeboat reached the becalmed trimaran *Blue Rose*, whose engine had failed. One of the trimaran's crew was taken aboard the lifeboat and, with the remaining crew member steering, the casualty was taken in tow to Sennen Cove.

At 4.14 p.m. on 10 October 1969, it was learnt that a fishing boat needed assistance three-quarters of a mile west-north-west of Tol Pedn. Seven minutes later *Susan Ashley* was launched. The lifeboat found the fishing boat *Antelope*, with a crew of four, at anchor with engine failure. The lifeboat towed the boat to Newlyn and was back at her station at 8.03 p.m.

During 1970 *Susan Ashley* performed only one effective service, on 16 July, when she saved three people who had been stranded by the tide. The following year she was called upon more often although the services were all somewhat routine in nature, beginning on 8 January 1971 when she helped the motor fishing vessel *Aquilon*, of Lorient. On 8 June 1971, at 8.11 p.m. the Coastguard informed the honorary secretary that a fishing boat with one person on board was in need of assistance six miles south-by-west of Cape Cornwall. *Susan Ashley* launched at 8.23 p.m.

in a light northerly breeze with a slight sea and found the fishing boat *T.G.S.*, fishing number PZ.96, just over a quarter of an hour later. At 8.43 p.m. a line had been secured aboard the vessel and the lifeboat towed her back to Sennen Cove. The two vessels arrived at 9.15 p.m. and the lifeboat rehoused after securing the fishing boat.

At 7.17 p.m. on 23 March 1972 the honorary secretary received a message from the Coastguard reporting that a flare had been seen from the yacht *Dogwatch* of Cowes. The yacht was a mile south of Longships and the coaster *Ability* was proceeding to investigate. At 7.55 p.m. a further message was received from the Coastguard requesting the services of the lifeboat as no other vessel was in a position to assist the yacht that was so close to the rocks. *Susan Ashley* launched at 8.05 p.m. and, half an hour later, reached the yacht which was two and a half miles south-west-by-west of the lifeboat station. One person was on board the yacht which had suffered engine failure. A line was secured and the lifeboat took her in tow to Newlyn where she was secured. The lifeboat returned to her station at 1.10 a.m. on 24 March.

By this time, *Susan Ashley* was reaching the end of her service life and, during 1972, a new lifeboat was allocated to Sennen Cove. *Susan Ashley* performed her final three services at Sennen during September 1972. On 7 September, at 3.52 a.m. the Coastguard informed the honorary secretary that red flares had been seen near Land's

Recovery of *Susan Ashley* in the shelter of the breakwater. (From an old postcard supplied by David Gooch)

Susan Ashley is hauled up the short slipway bow first. She will be rotated inside the boathouse on the turntable. To the right of her bow can be seen the remains of the slipway on which was laid the railway track used for launching during the 1920s. (From an old postcard supplied by David Gooch)

Coxswain Eric Pengilly (on the right) and Second Coxswain Maurice Hutchens stand in front of *Susan Ashley* with souvenirs from two of the ships aided by the Sennen lifeboat: five were saved from the trawler *Victoire Roger* on 24 March 1964; Penlee lifeboat *Solomon Browne* saved one and landed one body from *Juan Ferrer* on 23 October 1963. The casualty went in at Carn Boscawen near Tater Du lighthouse and, although Sennen Cove lifeboat was launched, she was not needed. (Derek Harvey)

After leaving Sennen Cove, *Susan Ashley* was stationed at Barry Dock until 1979 and in 1980 went to the National Lifeboat Museum in Bristol where she was displayed from 1980 until the mid-1990s. On arrival at Bristol she was repainted and subsequently kept in service condition, her engines being run periodically. She is pictured here during winter 1981-82. (Peter Barnfield)

Relief 37ft Oakley *Amelia* is launched on exercise. *Amelia* was on duty at Sennen from April to December 1973 during which time she is credited with saving two lives. She served in the relief fleet until 1978 and in November of that year was sent to Scarborough as station lifeboat. She remained there until 1991, launching more than a hundred times on service. (Peter Puddiphatt)

End and five minutes later requested lifeboat assistance. *Susan Ashley* proceeded towards Land's End and her crew saw the lights of the vessel in a small cove between very high cliffs. The bow of the casualty, the trawler *La Varenne*, of Cherbourg, was very close to the cliffs so the Coxswain approached with caution as numerous outlying rocks made the short passage hazardous. When they were closer to the casualty the lifeboatmen saw an inflatable raft alongside with four men aboard and the ship's boat hanging off with two men in it. A line was thrown to the raft and, with the ship's boat attached, this was hauled to the lifeboat through the very confused seas. The six men were quickly taken on board the lifeboat. As the rescued men were French and did not speak any English, it was indicated by sign language that two men were still aboard the trawler. Two of the lifeboatmen veered alongside the casualty in the ship's boat to pick up the last two men who were then transferred to the lifeboat. *Susan Ashley* was manoeuvred clear of the rocks with the raft and ship's boat in tow. The survivors were landed safely at Sennen Cove and the lifeboat rehoused at 6 a.m.

After this well executed rescue, *Susan Ashley* was in action again the following day. At 7.15 p.m. on 8 September, after the Coastguard had seen a yacht in distress two miles south of Longships lighthouse, the lifeboat was launched at 7.30 p.m. in a strong southerly breeze and slight sea. She found the casualty, the yacht *Titatam*, with the Isles of Scilly steamer RMS *Scillonian* standing by. The casualty had lost her rudder and, with two persons on board, was drifting. The lifeboatmen passed a tow line to the yacht and, once this was secured, towing commenced in worsening weather conditions. The casualty yawed extensively as she had no rudder making the tow slower and more difficult. Eventually, both lifeboat and yacht reached Newlyn harbour where the casualty was safely secured. *Susan Ashley* stayed in Newlyn overnight, returning to her station at 4.10 p.m. the following day.

She performed what proved to be her final service on 23 September, saving the yacht *Etam* and its three occupants. During the winter of 1972-73 she was not called upon and on 10 April 1973 left Sennen Cove for the last time after a quarter of a century of service. As the new lifeboat was not ready to take her place, *Susan Ashley* was temporarily replaced by the relief 37ft Oakley class lifeboat *Amelia* (ON.979).

During her short spell of just over six months at Sennen Cove, *Amelia* performed four effective services. The first of these took pace on 19 April 1973. At 8.52 p.m. the Coastguard informed the honorary secretary that the tug *Plato*, with the tug *Platina* in tow, required immediate assistance five miles south-by-west of the Longships lighthouse. *Amelia* was launched at 9.15 p.m. in a gentle to moderate north-easterly breeze. On arrival at the scene, the lifeboatmen found that the casualty's steering gear was disabled and the Trinity House vessel *Stella* was on the way to assist in towing. The lifeboat stood by until *Stella* had arrived and secured the tow line. Once the tow towards Mount's Bay had got under way, the lifeboat was released at 11.45 p.m. and returned to her station at 1.30 a.m. on 20 April.

The only life-saving service performed by *Amelia* took place on 19 August 1972. At 9.58 p.m. the Coastguard informed the station's Deputy Launching Authority that a rowing boat with two youths on board was in the vicinity of Carn Gloose and was unable to reach the shore. Ten minutes later, the lifeboat was launched in a calm wind and slight sea swell with an ebbing tide. Within ten minutes of launching, the lifeboat had reached the rowing boat and taken it in tow. Both boats reached the safety of Sennen Cove harbour and at 10.45 p.m. and the lifeboat was rehoused after landing the two survivors.

Diana White

The new lifeboat, destined to serve the station for almost two decades, was a 37ft 6in Rother class, a development of the successful 37ft Oakley class (of which the relief lifeboat *Amelia* was an example) but slightly larger and with better crew protection. The new boat's deck layout consisted of a long, watertight casing which stretched from the fore buoyancy chamber to the aft end of the engine room – almost the full length of the vessel. The enclosed fore cabin, with access through the engine room and an escape hatch through the roof, provided a watertight dry survivor cabin. Not only did the new design offer greater crew and survivor comfort than *Susan Ashley*, but she was self-righting by virtue of a watertight superstructure large enough to make her inherently unstable when capsized. A hollow wheelhouse roof was also incorporated into the design to aid self-righting. This almost fully enclosed cockpit was open only at the rear, although it was subsequently covered by a clear plastic screen for added crew protection. A radar scanner was fitted at the after end of the wheelhouse roof and hinged to swing down into a stowed position beneath the roofline to conform to the restricted headroom of the boathouse. The boat also carried MF radio, VHF/DF radio, echo-sounding equipment and a comprehensive range of other gear including a line-throwing pistol and breeches buoy.

The first Rother, named *Osman Gabriel* (ON.998), successfully completed her self-righting trial on 9 September 1972, was displayed at the Earl's Court Boat Show in London in January 1973 and entered service at Port Erin (Isle of Man) in July 1973. During the 1970s the RNLI placed orders for the construction of further Rother lifeboats and fourteen of the class were built in total between 1972 and 1982. The second Rother (ON.999) was allocated to Sennen Cove and was completed during 1973 at the Littlehampton boatyard of William Osborne Ltd. She arrived at Sennen in November 1973 and on 31 December 1973 *Amelia* departed.

The new Sennen lifeboat, provided from an anonymous gift together with the proceeds of the Cornish Lifeboat Appeal, was named *Diana White*. She was formally christened by HRH the Duke of Kent at a ceremony held at the lifeboat station on 19 July 1974. Earlier in the day, the Duke had visited the Lifeboat Exhibition at Plymouth being held to mark the 150th Anniversary of the RNLI's founding. He flew to Sennen by helicopter especially for the ceremony during which the new boat was delivered into the care of the Sennen Cove branch by Nigel Warrington Smyth, OBE, a vice-president of the RNLI, and she was accepted by the honorary secretary Captain H.B. Harvey. After the formal ceremony and service of dedication, the lifeboat was launched to the firing of three maroons and the Duke accepted the offer of an impromptu trip. He was taken to Land's End, steering the boat for some of the course himself, and then back to Sennen. About an hour after the Duke had left by

HRH the Duke of Kent is introduced to Sennen Cove lifeboatmen during the naming of *Diana White* on 19 July 1974. (By courtesy of RNLI Sennen Cove)

helicopter, the sea mist crept in, 'trapping in Sennen Cove the memory of a splendid royal occasion', as the RNLI's official account concluded.

The first service performed by *Diana White* took place on 15 April 1974, a couple of months before her official naming. After a member of the public informed the honorary secretary that a boat had fired flares off Sennen, *Diana White* was launched at 4.32 p.m. in a gentle easterly breeze and slight sea. She soon found the yacht *Magasu* two miles west-north-west of Sennen and out of fuel. The lifeboat towed the yacht to Newlyn harbour and returned to her station at 8.35 p.m. after a routine callout. This proved to be the only service of 1974 but, after no calls in 1975, the following year proved to be a busier one for *Diana White*.

The first launch of 1976 took place in the early hours of 8 June. Just after midnight the Coastguard informed the honorary secretary that flares had been observed eight miles to the north of the lifeboat station and *Diana White* was asked to investigate. Visibility was good, the wind was light and the sea was choppy when, at 12.32 a.m., *Diana White* was launched and proceeded towards the reported position of the casualty. She arrived on scene fifty minutes later and found the fishing vessel *Gillian Clair* with a crew of four on board. The vessel was at anchor as her propeller had been fouled by her own nets. With the tide at full flood, the lifeboat took the fishing vessel in tow and brought her into St Ives. *Diana White* then returned to her station, where she arrived at 6 a.m. but had to wait four hours until the tide permitted rehousing. The other three services of the year were all to fishing vessels in difficulty including, on 5 December, the French vessel *Gweer-Chez-Viari*, which was escorted to safety.

At 1.54 p.m. on 11 June 1977 the Coastguard informed the lifeboat station that a salvage vessel, on passage to Hayle, appeared to have stopped very close to the reef at the end of the slipway. At 2.28 p.m. the vessel fired a red flare and, just over ten minutes later, *Diana White* was launched and proceeded at full speed in squally weather with a strong north-north-westerly wind and very rough sea. At 2.45 p.m. the lifeboat arrived alongside the casualty, which was the motor vessel *Anniline*, of Leith, to find the vessel had suffered engine failure. She had anchored in a very perilous position close to rocks, directly down wind. A tow line was made fast and the lifeboat crew assisted in trying to raise the vessel's anchor. However, this proved impossible so the anchor chain had to be cut. The lifeboat proceeded to tow the vessel to Penzance harbour where *Anniline* was safely moored, enabling the lifeboat to return to her station. Following this difficult service, the vessel's owners made a donation to the local branch and crew.

On 1 August 1977, after receiving information that a small craft was in difficulty off Gwenver, *Diana White* was launched at 8.32 p.m. and proceeded to the scene at full speed. Within fifteen minutes of launching, the lifeboat arrived alongside the motor fishing vessel *Western Home*, of Penzance, with four people on board. The fishing vessel had sustained a broken shaft and had lost her propeller and, by the time the lifeboat arrived, was in the tidal race off the Brisons. The lifeboatmen passed a line to the vessel, enabling the lifeboat to tow the vessel to Newlyn harbour, which was reached at 11.36 p.m. Owing to the state of the tide, the lifeboat remained at Newlyn until 5.05 a.m. the following day when she left for the station. She arrived off the lifeboat slipway at 6.27 a.m. and was rehoused ready for service at 6.52 a.m.

The spectacular sight of *Diana White* launching down the slipway at Sennen Cove. (Peter Puddiphatt)

After two relatively routine calls, the next service in which *Diana White* was involved proved to be one of the most outstanding services in the station's history. Just before 7.15 p.m. on 16 November 1977 the honorary secretaries from both Sennen and St Ives lifeboat stations were informed by Land's End Coastguard that the 499-ton coaster *Union Crystal,* with a crew of six on board, was in trouble twelve miles north of Cape Cornwall. Her cargo of rock salt had shifted and she was listing. The onshore wind was coming from the north-west, strong gale to storm force nine to ten, with rain squalls and heavy seas. The St Ives lifeboat, the 37ft Oakley *Frank Penfold Marshall* (ON.992), was launched from her carriage into the harbour at 7.31 p.m. and set course for the casualty.

At Sennen Cove, a heavy swell from the north-west was breaking across the Cowloe Rocks less than 200 yards to the north west of the slipway and, with a four-knot tide running through The Tribbens channel, the honorary secretary, Captain Ewan Watson, was concerned about the severity of the sea off the slipway and had doubts about the safety of launching the lifeboat. However, after hearing from Land's End Coastguard that, at 7.19 p.m., a final message had been received from *Union Crystal* indicating that she was sinking, the honorary secretary and Coxswain/Mechanic, Eric Pengilly, fired the maroons and opened the boathouse doors to assess the conditions on the slipway. The scene from the top of the slipway was described as 'formidable at best'. A large north-west swell was falling heavily into the area across the lifeboat's launch path. Joined by the swell and tide running to the eastwards through the narrow neck of The Tribbens, the sea was described as 'mad' and a 'maelstrom' by launchers and local residents who had not witnessed conditions as bad for more than twenty years.

A fine photograph of *Diana White* at full speed. She served at Sennen Cove for almost twenty years and is credited with saving sixty-three lives during her time at the station. (Peter Puddiphatt)

Although the state of the sea clearly exceeded the limit for launching, by 7.30 p.m. Coxswain/Mechanic Pengilly had decided that they must try and he climbed aboard the lifeboat followed immediately by his crew, each man making a positive decision to go. It was a calculated risk which was undertaken purely out of a supreme sense of duty. At 7.33 p.m. *Diana White* was lowered down the slipway clear of the boathouse doors where she was held to allow Coxswain/Mechanic Pengilly time to observe the behaviour of the sea and try to establish some sort of pattern for predicting the right moment in which to launch. After ten minutes it became apparent that no such moment was likely to occur and so, at 7.43 p.m., the Coxswain gave the order and *Diana White* was launched.

As soon as she entered the water, the lifeboat was hit by short, steep waves as she began to turn to starboard. Her green light became fully open to onlookers on the slipway and it appeared she was about to be thrown on to the rocky shore by the continuous pounding of seas described by those present as 'mountainous'. Shore helpers standing at the top of the slipway rushed through the boathouse to the road and then along the beach certain that the boat was about to the driven ashore. Meanwhile, on board the lifeboat, Coxswain/Mechanic Pengilly was struggling hard to control the boat which, according to several eyewitnesses, 'stood on end' in the atrocious conditions. Acting Second Coxswain Maurice Hutchins and crew member Philip Shannon were standing either side of the Coxswain helping him to keep his position behind the wheel and get the wheel over as rapidly as possible.

Honorary secretary Captain Ewan Watson described seeing the lifeboat at this moment as she 'reared, plunged and twisted', appearing at one moment to actually be heading for the Cowloe rocks. But the tide swept her eastwards and, with crew members John Chope and John Pender looking aft and reporting the leading marks,

Emergency Mechanic Headley Hutchings looking out ahead and the one non-regular volunteer crew member, Cedric Johnson, in the radar seat, the three men behind the wheel finally succeeded in bringing the lifeboat's head to sea and she gained her leading marks. From then on, according to Captain Watson's description, she 'ploughed through the surf on the bar and then set off on her mission with nothing more than the comparative luxury of a force ten to contend with.'

At about 8 p.m. the Coastguard asked the tanker *Texaco Great Britain* to coordinate the vessels then on scene and both St Ives and Sennen lifeboats searched under her direction, together with other ships, illuminating the area from time to time with parachute flares and searchlights. At about 9.30 p.m. HMS *Penelope* arrived and was designated 'on scene' commander. Six ships, two lifeboats and two helicopters were now engaged in the search, with a Nimrod helicopter arriving at 10 p.m. At 10.34 p.m. the Nimrod sighted a life raft containing one survivor who was then picked up by helicopter. Thirteen minutes later a report from the helicopter stated that although six people had left the ship and all had been wearing lifejackets, only one life raft had been launched. After the fishing vessel *Pathfinder* found wreckage fifteen minutes later, the search area was moved north-eastwards.

At 11.17 p.m. *Diana White* was recalled to station as information to hand suggested there was virtually no hope of finding more survivors and the area was well covered by search craft. She could not return to Sennen and so made for Newlyn where she arrived at 1.20 a.m. on 17 November. At midnight, HMS *Diomede* arrived and took over as 'on scene' commander. She tasked the St Ives lifeboat to follow HMS *Penelope* and pick up as much of the wreckage as possible, which the lifeboat did with great efficiency. The lifeboatmen from St Ives recovered four life preservers as well as wreckage by the time she was finally stood down at 2 a.m., although she launched again at 9 a.m. to recover a body close inshore down the coast.

For their considerable efforts during this service, the Sennen lifeboatmen were formally recognised: the Silver medal was awarded to Coxswain Pengilly while the Thanks of the Institution Inscribed on Vellum was accorded to the other crew members: Maurice Hutchens, Philip Shannon, John Chope, Hedley Hutchings, John Pender and Cedric Johnson. Sadly, the medal was awarded posthumously as Eric Pengilly died in January 1978, a few weeks after the service. The Thanks on Vellum was also accorded to the St Ives Coxswain, Thomas Cocking snr, and the St Ives crew were presented with Vellum service certificates. Among the many letters received following this service was one from Captain James Summerlee, a pilot of British Airways Helicopters' Penzance to Isles of Scilly flight, who wrote of the Sennen Cove launch:

> May I, as a private individual, commend the integrity, skill and utmost bravery of those that took part ... conditions for a Sennen launch could not have been more hazardous. Having crossed that particular piece of sea some 20,000 times in the last thirteen years I can say I have never seen more violent weather and sea conditions. To decide to launch in those conditions because of the peril of other mariners takes incredible courage. To step aboard a lifeboat and go into such a sea requires even greater courage.

Following the death of Eric Pengilly, Maurice Hutchens was appointed as the new Coxswain/Mechanic. Pengilly had been Coxswain since 1968, having been Second Coxswain for three years previously. Originally a Coverack man, he had served in motor gun boats in secret missions to Norway and Sweden during the Second World War and as an RNLI Fleet Mechanic prior to his appointment as Coxswain. His successor was Sennen born and bred and had worked initially as a carpenter then as a fisherman and boatbuilder. He was Second Coxswain under Pengilly for nearly seven years but went back to fishing in 1973. He was appointed Coxswain in January 1978 and served in this post until his retirement in 1990.

One of the last launches in which Eric Pengilly was involved took place on 5 December 1977 in the relief 37ft Oakley lifeboat *Vincent Nesfield* (ON.994) on station in place of *Diana White,* which went to Mashford's Boatyard, Plymouth, for overhaul on 28 November 1977. During the early hours of 5 December, the Coastguard informed the honorary secretary that red flares had been seen to the south-west and also alerted two large stern trawlers that were at anchor in Whitesand Bay. The visibility was mainly good but the sea was rough and the wind was fresh to strong. At 1.44 a.m. *Vincent Nesfield* was launched and proceeded at full speed to the reported incident. At 2.15 a.m. the lifeboat crew saw a red flare ahead of them and, on investigation, found a life raft in which were two men. These two survivors, who were taken on board the lifeboat, reported that a second life raft had been launched from the casualty, which was the trawler *Boston Sea Ranger*, of Lowestoft. After a ten minute search, the lifeboatmen found the second life raft and took its sole occupant on board. All three survivors were then transferred to the stern trawler *Arctic Buccaneer*. Five men from *Boston Sea Ranger* were still unaccounted for and so the search continued with a helicopter and Nimrod aircraft assisting. After a while, a man

Diana White approaching the short slipway at Sennen ready to be recovered. (Peter Puddiphatt)

Bow-first recovery of *Diana White* up the short slipway. (Peter Puddiphatt)

in a life-jacket was picked up by the lifeboatmen and transferred to the comparative comfort of *Arctic Buccaneer*. Two more bodies were eventually picked up by other searching craft and at 9.30 a.m. the search was called off. Half an hour later the lifeboat returned to her station and was rehoused.

The only other effective service performed by *Vincent Nesfield* during her time on relief at Sennen took place on 18 February 1978. At 1.47 p.m. that day the Coastguard informed the honorary secretary that the catamaran *Floral Dancer*, of Falmouth, with three on board, was out of control in the vicinity of the Longships lighthouse and required assistance. Despite storm- to hurricane-force winds blowing from the south-east, with rain, hail and snow, visibility varied from a quarter to two miles when, at 2.18 p.m. *Vincent Nesfield* launched into the rough seas and proceeded at full speed towards the Longships. By this time a helicopter had arrived on the scene and found the casualty two miles west of the Brisons, well clear of the lee of the land. Guided by the helicopter, the lifeboat reached the casualty at 2.40 p.m. and found she had a fouled propeller and rudder. Her stays and halyards had been carried away and her other engine had failed, leaving her at the mercy of wind and tide. Because it was too risky to transfer the catamaran's three occupants on to the lifeboat, a tow line was passed and secured. The casualty was then towed into the relatively calmer waters close in under the land. The port hull was taking in water and, unless the vessel was quickly beached, she could be lost. She was therefore made fast to the starboard side of the lifeboat and a quick run was made for Sennen Cove harbour, an operation which involved steaming before storm- to hurricane-force winds right into the confined space of the harbour. However, the operation was successful and, at 4.20 p.m., the catamaran was beached without damage to either her or the lifeboat. As soon as the catamaran grounded, the securing lines were cut and the lifeboat went full astern immediately to save

Diana White off Land's End, summer 1981. (Peter Barnfield)

herself from being stranded by the rapidly falling tide. She then returned to station and was rehoused at 4.37 p.m.

Vincent Nesfield stayed at Sennen until *Diana White* returned on 16 April 1978. During her short spell at the Cove, the relief lifeboat is credited with saving six lives. The first service *Diana White* performed after her overhaul took place on 18 April, only two days after she had returned. She launched at 12.01 p.m., after local fisherman had informed the station that the fishing vessel *Sweet Sue* had suffered engine failure and become separated from the main fishing fleet. The fleet had returned to harbour as the weather deteriorated but *Sweet Sue* was long overdue and concern was felt for her safety. The weather was squally, although visibility was good; the north-westerly wind was freshening as the lifeboat proceeded into a moderate sea. Within fifteen minutes of launching, the lifeboat found the missing fishing vessel, three and a half miles north-north-west of the lifeboat station. She was making her way to port under her own power and so was escorted in by the lifeboat.

Less than two months after this service, on 14 June, *Diana White* went to the aid of another fishing vessel, *Deux Soeurs*, of Newlyn. The vessel was on fire off the Longships and the crew of three had taken to their life raft owing to the intensity of the blaze. The lifeboat launched at 11.22 p.m. and proceeded at full speed in good conditions, while her helicopter and other aircraft were already on scene. Twenty minutes after launching, the lifeboatmen found the casualty about a mile and a half south of the lifeboat station. The three survivors were taken off the life raft and onto the lifeboat and were landed at Sennen at 11.52 p.m.

During this period, as well as assisting fishing vessels in difficulty, the Sennen lifeboat frequently helped yachts in difficulty, such as *Agapanthus III* on 26 August 1979. At 4.20 a.m. the Coastguard informed the honorary secretary that the yacht had been struck by the trawling beams of a Belgian trawler and, having already suffered engine failure, was in need of assistance about four miles south of the station.

In good visibility and a gentle north-easterly breeze, *Diana White* was launched at 4.42 a.m. She reached the casualty within half an hour and found that her two metal masts were badly damaged and hanging over the starboard side leaving her helpless. She was taken in tow but, due to the swell and the casualty's list, the tow line severely chafed. However, the tow continued and, once calmer waters were reached, four lifeboatmen went on board in an attempt to clear the masts. The tow proceeded slowly until 4 p.m. when the casualty was safely moored and her crew of five landed. This difficult service had occupied the lifeboat crew for more than twelve hours by the time they rehoused the lifeboat.

During 1980, *Diana White* was called upon more often than any year hitherto. She performed seven effective services, the first on 4 March when she landed the body of a woman who had fallen over a cliff and then on 9 May when she assisted the fishing vessel *Bernadette Denise*, of Poole. On 16 May an incident took place in which lifeboat crew members were involved. A local council life guard, Nick Bryant, was painting his hut when he saw two swimmers a long way out to sea. He immediately put out on a surf-board and, on reaching the two swimmers, found they were indeed in difficulties, exhausted by the strength of the tide and coldness of the water. He towed them to Cowloe Rocks, which were nearer than the shore, and they clambered onto the rocks. Meanwhile, Second Coxswain John Pender had seen the swimmers in trouble and knew that help was required. Fortunately, a 9ft inflatable dinghy to be carried aboard *Diana White,* was already inflated and so Pender put out in this. He was then able to bring the two swimmers, who were visitors from Germany, ashore. One was suffering from hypothermia and exhaustion and was taken

Diana White bringing in the yacht *Lowly Worm* on 7 August 1986. The yacht and her crew of four were saved by the lifeboat. (Peter Puddiphatt)

to hospital by ambulance. For this service, letters of appreciation, signed by RNLI Director Rear Admiral W.J. Graham, were sent to Nick Bryant and Second Coxswain Pender.

On 2 August 1980 *Diana White* was called to the yacht *Philerise II* which had a disabled engine and was drifting helplessly on the ebb tide towards the Longships Reef in dead calm conditions. The tide had been ebbing for four hours when, at 1.34 a.m., *Diana White* launched. Within half an hour she was alongside the casualty. However, since restoring power to the yacht was impossible and gales were forecast, the only option was to tow the yacht to safety. Once a tow line had been rigged, the yacht was taken to St Ives where she was safely moored at 6.30 a.m., and by 8.45 a.m. *Diana White* was back at her station. On 14 October, she took a doctor to an injured man on board the tanker *Grey Fighter*, of London, and landed the individual concerned. The final service of the year took place on 28 December when the lifeboat assisted the Penzance fishing vessel *Shere Carn*.

At 11.30 p.m. on 2 May 1981 the Coastguard informed the honorary secretary that the yacht *Hidair*, of Barry Dock, had reported rudder trouble about five miles north of the station. They were monitoring the position and would advise if assistance was required. More than three hours passed until, at 2.55 a.m. on 3 May 1981, the Coastguard reported that the yacht's crew of six wished to abandon ship and so *Diana White* was launched. The lifeboat made good speed to the area but locating the casualty proved difficult because she had neither radar reflector nor any visible navigation lights. However, at 4.45 a.m. the lifeboat came alongside and found the yacht's crew all safe and well. Coxswain Maurice Hutchens decided to tow the yacht into Newlyn harbour, so a line was secured but the rudderless yacht proved difficult to tow so the lifeboat passed a thirty fathom warp and a couple of fenders to stream astern. With this deployed, both vessels were able to reach Newlyn harbour where the yacht was moored safely at 8.15 a.m. and her crew were landed. The lifeboat then returned to Sennen Cove.

On 19 September 1981, *Diana White* was involved in another medal-winning service of equal note to the *Union Crystal* launch described above. The Icelandic coaster *Tungufoss* was reported to be in distress four miles south of Longships Lighthouse by Land's End Coastguard who alerted the Deputy Launching Authority at Sennen Cove at 8.27 p.m. The coaster, with eleven men on board, was listing forty degrees to port after her cargo of maize had shifted in a south-westerly gale and very rough sea. At 8.45 p.m. *Diana White*, under the command of Coxswain Maurice Hutchens, was launched into a strong gale with winds force eight to nine. The moonlight provided some light and, between rain squalls, visibility was quite good; however, as the swell, which was coming from the south-west, hit the breakwater and passed over it, it created very heavy spray falling, thus reducing visibility. Once launched, the lifeboat's first leg, parallel to the beach, was downwind but severe motion was experienced by the crew as the boat turned to port and steamed at full speed across the wind making her seaward course down the leading marks.

After rounding Cowloe Rocks, *Diana White* soon cleared Land's End and *Tungufoss* finally came into view. The coaster's lights were still on and two other vessels, the coaster *Kilkenny* and the Norwegian tanker *Fiordshell*, were standing by. A Sea King helicopter scrambled from RNAS Culdrose arrived over the casualty at 9.17 p.m.

and, flying at 100ft with the wind averaging fifty-five to sixty knots but gusting to seventy knots, started the difficult and hazardous task of trying to lift the crew off the stern of the coaster. Although the helicopter's winchman was injured while bringing up the first survivor, two more men were picked up by flying the strop into the hands of other men waiting on the casualty.

When the lifeboat arrived on the scene at 9.39 p.m., the lifeboat crew ascertained that three men had been lifted off by helicopter and found another three had got into life rafts at the stern of the casualty, lying to starboard across wind and sea. But while manoeuvring to approach these life rafts, the stern of the lifeboat was overwhelmed by a wave which washed through her cockpit putting the radar out of action. Coxswain Hutchens' first attempts to approach the life rafts were unsuccessful and each time he had to go astern to prevent the lifeboat being carried dangerously close to the coaster's starboard quarter and propeller. Then, approaching from a different angle and keeping the lifeboat's bow to wind and sea, Coxswain Hutchens succeeded in making a satisfactory approach and he let the waiting crew aboard the coaster know that he was ready to take them off.

The crew assembled on the starboard quarter and one jumped into the first life raft. His companions slackened the painter of the rafts to allow them to ride clear of the stern and the lifeboat came in to snatch the man to safety. The rafts were then pulled back to the coaster's stern and, repeating the procedure, three men were successfully taken aboard the lifeboat in this way. However, as the life rafts filled with water, and with fewer men to help each time, the task of heaving them back to the coaster's stern became increasingly difficult. Two men tried to leap into the rafts, missed their footing and fell into the sea. At this point, the lights of the casualty had just gone out but, aided by the lights of the helicopter, Coxswain Hutchens was able to drop down wind and retrieve both men from the water.

Three men were still on *Tungufoss* which had now taken a list of sixty degrees. Coxswain Hutchens brought the lifeboat close in to the transom of the casualty using great skill in avoiding the rudder as the lifeboat rose and fell 20ft in the seas. One of the men slid down from the starboard alleyway and jumped onto the fore deck of the lifeboat to be received by the rescuers. A second man was taken off in the same manner as the lifeboat made another run in to the coaster's transom. By now the coaster was almost on her beam ends and as Coxswain Hutchens started his final approach the last man aboard, the master, climbed clear of the superstructure. It looked as though the vessel was about to founder and the Sea King helicopter, moving in ahead of the lifeboat, flew its lifting strop within reach of the waiting master. He managed to grab it and was lifted clear as the sea started to engulf him.

With all eleven of the crew safe, at 11.03 p.m. the lifeboat set a course for her station, while the casualty eventually foundered and sunk south of Gwennap Head. Despite very long following seas experienced in the gap between Longships and Land's End, the lifeboat made good progress and arrived at the slipway at 11.15 p.m. After refuelling and an inspection of some slight damage that had been incurred, the lifeboat was ready for service fifteen minutes after midnight on 20 September. Both the high degree of coordination between helicopter and lifeboat crews and also the fine discipline shown by those who were rescued contributed to the successful completion of this operation, despite the severe weather and the limited time available. The master, chief officer and some of the crew of the coaster visited the lifeboat house the next day to personally thank the Coxswain and crew and a telegram of thanks to all who had taken part in the rescue was received from the Iceland Steamship Company, owners of *Tungufoss*.

For this outstanding rescue, during which the lifeboat was taken in to *Tungufoss* approximately twenty times as the coaster heeled over further and further, the Silver medal was awarded to Coxswain Hutchens in recognition of his courage, leadership and excellent seamanship; Medal Service Certificates were presented to the rest of the crew: Second Coxswain John Pender and crew members Cedric V. Johnson, Timothy M. George, Derek Angrove, Philip C. Shannon, Terrance W. Green. A letter signed by Rear Admiral W.J. Graham, Director of the RNLI, and addressed to Captain R.C. Dimmock, Commanding Officer of the Royal Naval Air Station Culdrose, expressed the RNLI's appreciation to the helicopter pilot and his crew.

Recognition for the Sennen lifeboatmen's achievements came from Iceland as well. In a letter to the RNLI, Mr G. Fridriksson, director of the National Lifesaving Association of Iceland, wrote:

> The whole Icelandic people is full of admiration for the heroic rescue action by which the lives of the *Tungufoss* crew were so miraculously saved, and we are all deeply grateful to the helicopter and lifeboat crews who, at the risk of their own lives, participated in the operation. On behalf of the National Lifesaving Association I would like you to convey our deep-felt thanks to all those who made the rescue possible.

On 17 February 1982, at a special ceremony held at London's Hyde Park Hotel, the President of Iceland, Mrs Vigdis Finnbogadottir, presented the Republic of Iceland's Silver Medal for valour (the country's highest bravery award) to Coxswain Hutchens, all members of the lifeboat's crew as well as the helicopter crew. Mrs Finnbogadottir said that the medal, instituted in 1950, had only been awarded once

Diana White on the short slipway being recovered. (Peter Puddiphatt)

before and added that the people of Iceland '... will never forget what you did, and what you do. I wish you to wear the medals often, because then I wish you long life.' Presentations were also made by the Iceland Steamship Company and the National Lifesaving Association of Iceland. The most touching speech came from Gunnar Thorsteignsson, Captain of the coaster, who was lifted off his vessel only minutes before she sank. With his crew, the captain had bought thick woollen Icelandic sweaters for the lifeboatmen, helicopter crew and coastguards 'for saving our lives'. In his perfect English he expressed his thanks but just his presence was enough to remind everybody that, without the helicopter and the Sennen Cove lifeboat, he would not have been alive.

Three months after the *Tungufoss* service, the relief 37ft Oakley *Vincent Nesfield*, temporarily on station again in place of *Diana White*, was launched during one of the most tragic incidents ever to befall Cornwall's lifeboat communities. On 19 December 1981 the Penlee lifeboat *Solomon Browne* (ON.954) put out on service to the motor vessel *Union Star* in a severe storm, one of the worst to hit the Cornish coast. During their gallant attempts to save the motor vessel's crew, the Penlee lifeboat's entire crew of eight, together with the eight crew on board the motor vessel, all perished and the lifeboat was completely wrecked. At Sennen, Coxswain Maurice Hutchens heard reports of the operation on his radio scanner and, when it became clear that the attempted rescue from the coaster was not straightforward, went to the lifeboat house and started assembling a crew. In the southerly gale, the Cove was relatively calm and launching the relief lifeboat was straightforward; however, travelling south, out of the shelter of the land, they met the full force of the weather as they attempted to pass Land's End in truly appalling conditions. The passage around Land's End, where two tides meet in an area of confused water, threw up particularly heavy seas. As soon as she rounded Land's End, *Vincent Nesfield* hit the oncoming waves and at one point began to climb a vertical wall of water in the darkness. As the lifeboat crested the wave and dropped into the trough, Coxswain Hutchins decided to turn around as progress was impossible and it was obvious he could not offer any assistance to those in difficulty. While the nation as a whole was stunned by this incident, the awfulness of the tragedy was felt particularly keenly throughout Cornwall's lifeboat communities. For Coxswain Hutchens, turning back because of the force of the weather, when friends and colleagues were in trouble, was probably one of the hardest decisions he had ever made.

Vincent Nesfield searched for a missing crewman from the cargo vessel *Mark*, of Panama, on 28 December 1981 and managed to recover a life raft. *Diana White* returned to station on 15 May 1982 and performed one service during the summer. At 10 a.m. on 17 June 1982 a report was received that a small yacht had a broken mast in the vicinity of Wolf Rock lighthouse and required assistance. In near gale-force winds and rough seas, *Diana White* launched at 10.24 a.m. and proceeded to the south but was unable to locate the casualty. A Nimrod aircraft was called in and saw the yacht's red flare at 11.58 a.m. about thirteen miles north-west of the lifeboat. Just over an hour later, the lifeboat reached the casualty, the yacht *Greenburrow*, of Bosham, with two persons on board. *Diana White* then proceeded to escort the yacht, which was using its auxiliary engine, to a sheltered anchorage in Sennen Cove where the lifeboat crew assessed the situation. After the lifeboat crew had taken a meal, the casualty was towed to Newlyn harbour in the evening and secured there at 9 p.m. The owner of the yacht made a generous donation to the crew in appreciation of this service.

Although her services were required most often to help yachts and fishing boats in trouble, occasionally *Diana White* was called to assist larger vessels, such as *Tungufoss*, and, on 2 April 1983, a ferry. At 7.12 a.m. that day, the honorary secretary was informed that Brittany Ferries' car/passenger ferry *Armourique*, on a routine crossing to Cork, was off Pendeen with many passengers affected by fumes from a fire in the vessel's furnishings. Helicopters were ready to take off the most serious casualties and the lifeboat was asked to stand by. So, at 8.40 a.m., *Diana White* launched and proceeded to a position approximately two miles west-south-west of the Longships. The casualty headed for Mount's Bay, where the lifeboat met her and, as soon as she was anchored, the lifeboat went alongside. The station's Honorary Medical Adviser went aboard to assist the Port Medical Officer. The lifeboat then took on board the Culdrose fire crew and their equipment, a body and twenty passengers affected by smoke who needed hospital treatment. All were landed for treatment at Penzance and, on a second trip, the lifeboat took ten further passengers off. At 2.28 p.m., the lifeboat was released from service and proceeded to Newlyn. However, just over half an hour later she was recalled and stood by the casualty until 5.15 p.m. As no further passengers needed treatment, the lifeboat was finally released and returned to station, where she was rehoused at 7.15 p.m.

During 1985, *Diana White* was called on to perform more routine services, including escorting two fishing vessels on 16 March and helping the motor cruiser *My Haven* on 17 April. The most tragic incident of the year, and in fact the most tragic Diana White was involved in while at Sennen, took place on 6 May 1985. A party of children from Stoke Poges Middle School were visiting Land's End whilst on a trip to West Cornwall. Unaware of the danger of the waves off the rocks, some of the children ventured too close and four of the youngsters were washed into the sea. The crew of *Diana White* carried out a long and thorough search but sadly their efforts were in vain as Nicholas Hurst (aged ten), Robert Ankers (eleven), Ricci Lamden (eleven) and Jamie Holloway (eleven) were never found. The parents of the four lads started a fund in memory of their lost sons and raised almost £100,000 which was donated to the RNLI in recognition of the efforts made by the crew of the Sennen Cove lifeboat that day and to help fund the station's next lifeboat.

The next call for *Diana White* was more straight forward and had a more positive outcome. On 18 May 1985, at 7.31 p.m., the owner of Sennen Cove Hotel informed the honorary secretary that a boat had overturned by the Cowloe Rocks, a mile west of the station, in a gentle north-easterly breeze. The lifeboat launched three minutes later into a slight sea with a heavy swell and found the sole survivor from the fishing boat *Sarah Jane*. He was picked up and landed ashore while his boat sank.

On 7 August 1986, the Coastguard informed the honorary secretary that flares had been seen ten miles north-west of Cape Cornwall just before 4 a.m. A gale from the west-north-west was making the sea rough when *Diana White* launched at 4.07 a.m. and set course for the area. At 5.16 a.m. contact was made with HMS *Andromeda* to the north of the casualty and then a D/F fix was made on the casualty, the yacht *Lily of the Valley* with four persons on board. At 5.40 a.m. the lifeboat reached the yacht and came alongside to pass a tow line. The casualty was then taken through the heavy seas round

Relief 37ft 6in Rother *The Davys Family* (ON.1064) at the head of the slipway while on temporary duty during 1987. *Diana White* was being replanked at Mashford's Boatyard, Plymouth, while *The Davys Family* stood in from 21 December 1986 until 30 March 1988. (Peter Puddiphatt)

Diana White in the water at Mashford's Boatyard, Cremyll, near Plymouth, on 28 March 1988 after her extensive refit and just before she returned to Sennen. (Tony Denton)

Land's End to Newlyn Harbour. Both lifeboat and yacht reached the safety of the harbour at 10 a.m. An hour and a half later the lifeboat left for her station, where she arrived at 1 p.m. and was placed on moorings before being rehoused three hours later.

Diana White was called into action later in the year. On 13 September at 2.13 p.m., the Coastguard informed the honorary secretary that a catamaran was in difficulties eight miles north of Pendeen light. In heavy rain, an easterly gale and rough seas, *Diana White* launched at 2.25 p.m. and proceeded to search for the casualty which was not found at the given position and was sending only very weak radio signals. Eventually the casualty was spotted by a French fishing boat, much further to the north, so the lifeboat set a new course. An hour after launching, she reached the catamaran *Joint Assets* eighteen miles north of Pendeen light. On board was a single occupant who was tired and cold. A lifeboatman went on board the catamaran to secure a tow line and the vessel was then towed to Sennen Cove where it was anchored at 9 p.m. The lifeboat remained on her moorings until 11 p.m., by which time sufficient water enabled her to be recovered.

This rescue was to be the last that *Diana White* undertook for more than a year as, on 21 December 1986, she was taken to Mashford's Boat Yard, Plymouth, where extensive work was undertaken to replank her hull. This took more than a year to complete and she did not return to Sennen until March 1988. She was relieved by another 37ft 6in Rother, *The Davys Family* (ON.1064), built in 1981 and originally stationed at Shoreham Harbour, which launched on service four times during her stay at Sennen. Her first service took place in the early hours of 16 June and proved to be a particularly long one. She launched at 5 a.m. with a doctor on board to help a sick crewman on board the fishing vessel *Galwad-y-Mor*, twenty-eight miles north-west of Longships lighthouse. The fishing vessel was reached at 6.25 a.m. and the doctor was transferred from the lifeboat. After examining and treating the sick man, he was taken on board the lifeboat together with the sick man and both were brought ashore at Sennen at 8.15 a.m. The sick man was taken to hospital by ambulance and the lifeboat returned to station.

The Davys Family performed two services during March 1988. On 14 March she launched during the late evening to assist the fishing vessel *J.B.*, of Brixham, which was taking in water nine miles west-north-west of Pendeen. The lifeboat was launched at low water and proceeded to locate the casualty by D/F radio. At 9.20 p.m. the fishing vessel was reached and, after a pump had been brought out to the vessel by helicopter, the fishing vessel was able to increase her speed from about two knots to six knots. The lifeboat escorted her to Newlyn where she arrived at 3 a.m. on 15 March. As the forecast gale and heavy rain had arrived, the lifeboat stayed overnight and did not return to Sennen until 2.45 p.m. on 15 March.

Ten days later she was out again, launching at 5.05 a.m. to assist the Cypriot cargo vessel *Retriever*, with six persons on board. The vessel's cargo had shifted in a severe south-westerly gale and very rough sea four miles east of Sevenstones. *The Davys Family* arrived on scene at 6.28 a.m. and escorted the vessel to a position ten miles north of St Ives; she then anchored at St Ives to await an improvement in the weather and tidal conditions before returning to Sennen at 1.50 p.m.

Diana White returned from the Plymouth boatyard, where she had spent the past year, at the end of March 1988 and was soon in action, performing two services the following month both involving towing yachts to Newlyn. On 22 April 1988, the Coastguard informed the honorary secretary at 11.11 p.m. that the yacht *Katy* had a fouled propeller and, with four persons on board, was taking in water four miles west of Pendeen light. A strong easterly gale was making the sea choppy when, at 11.29 p.m., the lifeboat launched and proceeded to locate the casualty using D/F radio. At 12.25 a.m. on 23 April the yacht was found and two lifeboatmen went aboard to assess the situation. A heavy rope was around the propeller so, using a tow line, the casualty was slowly pulled around head to wind, taking the pressure off the rope causing the fouling. When the casualty's engine was reversed, the rope was cleared from the propeller. In view of the weather conditions with a gale-force wind, Coxswain Hutchens decided to tow the yacht around Land's End to Newlyn and the two boats reached the safety of Newlyn harbour at 4 a.m. The lifeboat remained there until 6 a.m. and then returned to station to be rehoused at 8 a.m.

The next service took place on 30 April when, at 3.32 p.m., the yacht *Tia*, with four persons on board, was reported to be drifting with a fouled propeller five miles north-west of Pendeen Light. *Diana White* launched at 3.41 p.m. into a strong south-easterly breeze gusting to near gale force and proceeded to locate the casualty using VHF/DF radio. An hour after launching she reached the casualty and found its propeller fouled with a net but the crew had managed to clear the steering gear. The yacht was taken in tow and, in deteriorating weather, brought to Newlyn harbour. During the tow, which lasted almost eight hours, the weather deteriorated further with the wind gusting to strong gale force and the lifeboat stopped in sheltered water at Sennen Cove to check the seaworthiness of the yacht. *Diana White* remained in Newlyn for the tide change and sufficient water at the Cove before returning to station to be rehoused at 3.20 a.m. having been away on service for twelve hours.

In 1989, *Diana White* performed five services, all routine in nature. On 3 April, she launched to assist the yacht *Legend* which was dismasted and had no engine three miles south-south-west of Gwennap Head. The station's Honorary Medical Advisor and another lifeboatman were put on board the casualty to care for the yacht's sick crew. The yacht was then towed out of the bad weather to Sennen Cove, where the two sick survivors were landed and she was subsequently taken to the shelter of Penzance Dock.

On 30 May, after the honorary secretary had been informed that the motor fishing vessel *Confide*, with five persons on board, was taking in water six miles west of Gwennap Head, *Diana White* launched at 9.18 p.m. to go to her aid. She reached the casualty an hour later and stood by as a helicopter lowered a portable pump down on to the vessel, together with a pump operator. This pump contained the leak so the operator was transferred onto the lifeboat and then lifted back into the helicopter. The lifeboat escorted the casualty until it had a second pump running and was approaching Newlyn. With the safety of the casualty confirmed, the lifeboat returned to station and rehoused at 11.05 p.m.

The next service of 1989 took place on 28 June when *Diana White* assisted the yacht *Cariad-y-Mor*, with two persons on board, which had suffered steering failure three miles north-west of Pendeen. The lifeboat reached the casualty at 1.51 p.m. and took off one sick and frightened survivor. Two lifeboatmen were put aboard the yacht to assist with a tow, which proved very difficult as the lifeboat was continually sheering in the fresh north-westerly wind and choppy seas. During the tow, the yacht's mast came down but did not cause any injuries and the yacht was handed over to the St Ives Authority together with the two survivors.

On 23 July, the lifeboat assisted the yacht *Huff*, of Arklow, which was damaged and becalmed to the north of Longships. The vessel was towed to Sennen Cove where repairs were affected. The final service of the year took place on 22 November when *Diana White* assisted the fishing vessel *Celtic Crusader*, in difficulty two miles south-west of Longships, and escorted her to Newlyn.

On 10 January 1990, *Diana White* launched at 7.29 a.m. to the yacht *Shortwave*, which required assistance three miles north-west of Pendeen. In a south-westerly force four to five wind, the yacht was escorted to the safety of St Ives. This service proved to be the last for Coxswain Maurice Hutchens, who retired in April 1990 after twelve years in the post. The first service under the new Coxswain, Terry George, took place on 26 May. *Diana White* was launched at 8.17 a.m. to assist the Swedish yacht *Treviljor* which was dismasted south of the Longships lighthouse in force six to seven easterly winds that caught out many vessels around the coasts. The Sennen lifeboatmen assisted in clearing fouled rigging and the yacht was then towed to Newlyn harbour in a routine first service for Coxswain George.

During July 1990 *Diana White* performed four services, the first of which took place on 5 July and proved to be a difficult one undertaken in heavy seas. At 11.30 a.m. that day, the Coastguard notified the station that a Swiss-registered yacht had lost her steering about a mile north of Pendeen. *Diana White* was launched just nine minutes later and set out for the yacht's last reported position. With the wind from the north-north-west at force seven to eight and a 10ft to 12ft sea swell running, the yacht *Koo-She* was off a very dangerous lee shore. Although the helicopter arrived on the scene shortly before the lifeboat, it did not take off any of the yacht's crew as the lifeboat was just minutes away. At 12.05 p.m. the lifeboat located the yacht which was now little more than a quarter-of-a-mile off the rocks near Botallack. A tow was quickly passed to the casualty and the lifeboat began to ease the yacht away to seaward and clear of the shore. Because of the weather conditions, it was necessary for the lifeboat to head offshore to clear Land's End and the Runnelstone and to pass Sennen Cove to find shelter behind the land from the westerly seas. 'The crucial part of the rescue was the onshore wind,' Coxswain Terry George explained later, adding, 'we eased him off very gently into the weather to get a bit of sea room'.

The lifeboat then headed for Newlyn where the yacht, with four crew on board, was safely moored in the harbour after a tow that had lasted almost four hours. After securing *Koo-She*, which had been sailing from Norway to St Malo via Spitzbergen and Shetland, *Diana White* immediately left for Sennen where, although conditions were very bad with seas breaking over the harbour wall, the lifeboat was successfully recovered and was ready for service again by 6.05 p.m. Following this service, a letter of appreciation from the Chief of Operation of the RNLI was sent to Coxswain George and the crew comprising John Pender, Chris Angove, Richard Manser, Phil Shannon, Derek Angove, and Timmy George, in recognition of their efforts during this difficult operation undertaken in gale-force winds.

The other services of the month also proved to be demanding on both lifeboat and crew. On 19 July at 11.39 p.m. *Diana White* was launched to assist the 1,500-ton cargo

Terry George, Coxswain of the
Sennen Cove lifeboat since 1989.
(By courtesy of the RNLI)

vessel *Rocquaine* which had an engine room fire and was stranded five miles north–west of the Longships lighthouse. A helicopter from RNAS Culdrose was also scrambled and the lifeboat stood by throughout the night while attempts were made to bring the fire under control. Eventually, the cargo vessel's crew flooded the engine room with carbon dioxide to put the fire out. The vessel was then taken in tow by the Irish Lights vessel *Grey Seal*, which was in the area, and the lifeboat began the journey back to Sennen after being out all night. However, on her way back to Sennen, *Diana White* was tasked to assist the motor boat *Albatross*, which had fouled its propeller in mid-channel and was under tow by a Dutch cargo vessel. The lifeboat took over the tow and then brought the boat, with three men and three women on board, into Newlyn harbour. The lifeboat finally returned to station at 2.20 p.m. on 20 July.

Ten days later, on 30 July 1990, *Diana White* performed her final service of the month, although it proved to be a false alarm with good intent. She launched at 11.59 a.m. following a report of a fishing boat in difficulties close under Land's End, but none of the boats found seemed to be in difficulty.

On 21 March 1991, *Diana White* was involved in a major passenger-ferry disaster exercise in Mount's Bay, south of Penzance, in which the Penlee and Lizard lifeboats were also involved. The exercise, which involved the evacuation of over 280 volunteers from the Isle of Scilly passenger-ferry *Scillonian III*, was organized by HM Coastguard to demonstrate the ability of the CG Rescue Coordination Centre at Falmouth, together with other emergency services, to deal successfully with all aspects of a passenger-ferry disaster. The RAF's Rescue Coordination Centre at Plymouth was also involved, together with helicopters from RNAS Culdrose, the Police, Fire and Ambulance services and the exercise passed off successfully.

In April 1991, soon after this exercise, *Diana White* left Sennen Cove for the final time. She was taken to Falmouth Boat Company where she stayed until September. On 18 September 1991 she left Falmouth for the RNLI Depot, Poole, arriving the following day, where she was kept in storage until June 1992. She was then sold to New Zealand for further service as a lifeboat with the Sumner Lifeboat Institution.

Diana White moored at the RNLI
Depot, Poole, in October 1991
after being replaced at Sennen
Cove. (Paul Russell)

To reach her new homeland she was taken by road to Southampton on 15 June 1992 for shipment on board a P&O Lines vessel on 19 June. She was offloaded at Lyttelton, New Zealand, on 5 August 1992 and immediately launched amid great excitement amongst the Sumner lifeboat supporters. She replaced another former RNLI lifeboat, the 35ft 6in Liverpool class *Rescue III* (ON.914, ex-*Tillie Morrison, Sheffield II*), which was subsequently sold by the Sumner Institution. *Diana White* was then accompanied by the other two rescue boats at Sumner, jetboat *Caroline Nicholson* and IRB *Lady Frances*, on trials in the bay.

On 8 November 1992, she was formally christened *Joseph Day* by Dame Catherine Tizard, Governor General of Christchurch, and officially began her new career as a lifeboat in New Zealand. She retained her original 52hp Thornycroft diesels throughout her time with the Sumner Institution and was maintained to a very high standard. She was replaced by another former RNLI lifeboat, *Helmut Schroder of Dunlossit* (ex-ON.1032), in August 1998 and was put up for sale. In 2001 she was sold for approximately NZ$55,000 to a private owner who moved her to Taurananga, Bay of Plenty, and reverted to her original name of *Diana White*.

Right above: Diana White out of the water at the RNLI Depot, Poole, awaiting disposal. (Phil Weeks)

Right middle: Diana White is positioned onto the low-loader to be taken by road to Southampton on 15 June 1992 for shipment on board a P&O container ship.

Below: Renamed *Joseph Day* for service with the Sumner Lifeboat Institution, *Diana White* with her replacement at Sumner, the former RNLI 50ft Thames class lifeboat *Helmut Schroder of Dunlossit*, which arrived in Lyttelton, New Zealand, on 9 October 1998 having served at the Islay lifeboat station from 1979 until 1997. (Supplied by Tim Stevens)

5

Fast lifeboats come to Sennen

On 9 April 1991, the relief 37ft 6in Rother *Harold Salvesen* (ON.1022) arrived at Sennen from Anglesey Boat Company in Beaumaris, via Holyhead, Fishguard and Padstow, in place of *Diana White*. She stayed until 9 October 1991 and performed a number of routine rescues while on duty. On 15 April she was launched at 3 p.m. to assist the fishing vessel *Scarlet Thread*, which was reported to be taking in water four miles north-west of the Wolf Rock. A pump was placed aboard the vessel by rescue helicopter and the lifeboat then towed the vessel to Newlyn harbour. Further services, all of a routine nature, followed throughout the summer. On 4 May, *Harold Salvesen* assisted the fishing vessel *La Belle Bretagne* in a northerly force six with a moderate to rough sea. On 15 July, she went to the French yacht *Alioth III* which was located by a rescue helicopter three miles south of the Runnelstone. She reached the yacht at 7.50 a.m. and found two cold and distressed female crew members who were taken on board the lifeboat, which then escorted the casualty to Newlyn. On 1 August, *Harold Salvesen* recovered a body from the sea at Boat Cove, Pendeen, and on 27 August performed what proved to be the last service carried out by a Rother

Relief 37ft 6in Rother *Harold Salvesen* (ON.1022) exercising with a Royal Navy Sea King helicopter off Land's End during the station's annual lifeboat day, 1991. *Harold Salvesen* was the last Rother at Sennen, launching on service six times. She served from 9 April to 9 October 1991, part of which time she was on moorings while the boathouse was altered for the 12m Mersey. (Sennen Cove Lifeboat Archive)

12m Mersey class lifeboat

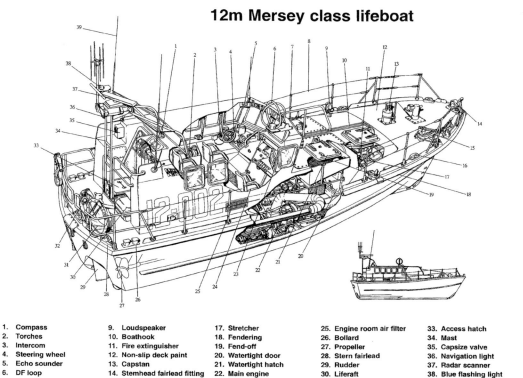

1. Compass	9. Loudspeaker	17. Stretcher	25. Engine room air filter	33. Access hatch
2. Torches	10. Boathook	18. Fendering	26. Bollard	34. Mast
3. Intercom	11. Fire extinguisher	19. Fend-off	27. Propeller	35. Capsize valve
4. Steering wheel	12. Non-slip deck paint	20. Watertight door	28. Stern fairlead	36. Navigation light
5. Echo sounder	13. Capstan	21. Watertight hatch	29. Rudder	37. Radar scanner
6. DF loop	14. Stemhead fairlead fitting	22. Main engine	30. Liferaft	38. Blue flashing light
7. Stanchion	15. Anchor	23. Radar	31. Drogue	39. Whip aerial
8. Guard wires	16. Drougue fairlead	24. Seat	32. Breeches buoy	

Cutaway drawing of 12m Mersey class lifeboat. This RNLI publicity drawing, produced as the first Merseys were coming into service, shows 12-002, the second of the class, which was stationed at Hastings and named *Sealink Endeavour*.

class lifeboat at Sennen Cove when she launched at 3.26 p.m. to assist a small inflatable being blown out to sea from Sennen Beach and brought the craft back to Sennen beach.

While these services were taking place, a new 12m Mersey class all-weather lifeboat had been under construction for Sennen. The Mersey class was developed during the 1980s for stations where the lifeboat needs to be launched off a carriage and was intended to replace 37ft Oakley and 37ft 6in Rother lifeboats which were reaching the end of their operational lives. To enable the boat to be launched from a beach, the propellers had to be protected and this was achieved by the hull form which incorporated a tunnel-stern and extended bilge keels that supported the weight of the boat on the beach, preventing propellers and rudders from damage. The hull arrangement was also suitable for slipway launching. The Mersey was capable of a speed of more than seventeen knots (twice that of the old designs), powered by twin 285hp Caterpillar 3208T turbo-charged diesel engines, carried a crew of six and fitted with the latest navigation and communication equipment. Approximately 245 gallons of fuel were carried giving a range at full speed of 145 nautical miles. The design was self-righting by virtue of the inherent buoyancy of the watertight wheelhouse, which also contained permanent seating for the crew, with an additional seat for a doctor. The first boats of the new class were constructed from aluminium but later boats were made from fibre reinforced composite (FRC).

Following the introduction of the Mersey into the RNLI's fleet in the late 1980s, a target date of 1993 was set by when it was intended to have 'fast' lifeboats operating from every station equipped with an all-weather lifeboat. This, of course, included Sennen Cove. In considering a replacement for the Rother at Sennen, the new Mersey design was seen as the most suitable choice as it could be slipway launched and was of a similar size to the Rother thus negating the need for extensive alterations to the boathouse. In November 1990 the RNLI announced that a new Mersey was to be sent to the station in late summer the following year. To accommodate her, the boathouse and slipway had to be altered and while this work was undertaken *Harold Salvesen* was kept on moorings.

The Four Boys

The hull of the new Mersey lifeboat allocated to Sennen was moulded of FRC by Green Marine, Lymington, and this was then taken to Cowes, Isle of Wight, where it was fitted out at FBM Ltd, at a total cost of approximately £455,000. The new boat was partly funded by money raised trough a campaign organized by the parents of the four boys, pupils of Stoke Poges Middle School, who were swept off rocks at Land's End in May 1985 while on a trip with their school (see p.86). Further money raised by the Sennen Cove Lifeboat Appeal was put towards the cost of the lifeboat, which was the nineteenth Mersey class to be built, and the name *The Four Boys* was chosen for the vessel in memory of Nicholas Hurst, Robert Ankers, Ricci Lamden and Jamie Holloway. During November 1991, while the newly-completed craft was at the RNLI Depot, in Poole, the parents of the four boys visited to see the boat themselves and to hand over a cheque from their fund-raising efforts since the tragedy.

The Four Boys leaving Fowey harbour in November 1991 on passage to Sennen. (Paul Richards)

1   The lifeboat house with two slipways constructed in 1927-29 pictured from the breakwater at low tide. (Nicholas Leach)

2   The 1927-29 lifeboat house seen from the south. This photograph gives a good indication of the sheer size of the boathouse, built to such dimensions that, on the turntable inside, the lifeboat could be turned through 360 degrees. (Nicholas Leach)

3   *Susan Ashley* at the head of the long slipway. (Derek Harvey)

4   *Diana White* in the Cove with the lifeboat house and slipways. (Peter Puddiphatt)

5   *Diana White* at the foot of the short slipway being readied for recovery. (Peter Puddiphatt)

6   Relief 37ft Oakley *Vincent Nesfield* at the head of the long slipway while *Diana White* is recovered up the short slipway after returning from refit in May 1982. *Vincent Nesfield* had been on relief since October 1981 while *Diana White* had been at Falmouth Boat Company for survey. (Peter Puddiphatt)

7   Relief 37ft 6in Rother *The Davys Family* being recovered after exercise. Originally built for service at Shoreham Harbour, she was placed in the Relief Fleet in December 1986 and came to Sennen on 21 December 1986. While *The Davys Family* was on station, *Diana White* went for an extensive overhaul, not returning to station until April 1988. (Peter Puddiphatt)

8   *The Four Boys* is launched down the long slipway. She was one of only four 12m Merseys to be operated from slipway stations as most boats of the class were launched from a carriage. (Peter Puddiphatt)

9 A fine view of *The Four Boys* seen from the cliffs at Penberth Cove, July 1998. (Tim Stevens)

10 *The Four Boys* is launched on 19 July 1998 to go to Penberth Cove Lifeboat Day, a regular fund-raising event in the station's calendar. (Tim Stevens)

11 *The Four Boys* served at Sennen Cove from 1991 to 1998. (By courtesy of Rick Tomlinson)

14   *Above*: D Class inflatable *Spirit of the ACC* (D-490) makes a spectacular sight as she crosses the breaking waves while on exercise just off Sennen Beach in 1997. On board are helmsman Dan Shannon with crew members Andrew Tonkin (port side) and John Thomas (starboard side). (Tim Stevens)

12   *Opposite above:* Relief 12m Mersey *Lifetime Care* on exercise, 27 June 1995. The relief lifeboat stood in for *The Four Boys* between May and September 1995. (Tim Stevens)

13   *Opposite below:* D Class inflatable *Spirit of the ACC* (D-490), sent to Sennen Cove in March 1996. The boat was funded by The Royal Logistic Corps with various contributions from other military regiments, one of several inshore lifeboats so funded. (Tim Stevens)

15   *The Four Boys* brings the yacht *Nyota* into Newlyn harbour on 16 May 1992 after finding her in difficulty a mile west of Longships. (Peter Puddiphatt)

16   12m Mersey *The Four Boys*, on station at Sennen Cove from 1991 to 1998, leads the flotilla of RNLI operational lifeboats during the RNLI's 175th anniversary celebrations at Poole in June 1999. (Nicholas Leach)

17 *The Four Boys* at the end of a rainbow whilst on her moorings for the last time in the Cove, 5 December 1998. (Tim Stevens)

18   *Norman Salvesen* returning to her station after exercise, 25 May 1999, and preparing to be recovered. (Tim Stevens)

19   Recovery of *Norman Salvesen* after exercise, 25 May 1999. She has been the only motor lifeboat to be recovered stern first via the unique double slipway arrangement at Sennen. (Tim Stevens)

20   47ft Tyne *Norman Salvesen* and Sennen lifeboat crew at the head of the slipway for the rededication of the lifeboat on 29 June 1999 at the Harbour Beach. (Paul Richards)

21   *Norman Salvesen* on exercise in calm seas. Built in 1988, she served at Wick in the north of Scotland for almost a decade before coming to Sennen. (Tim Stevens)

22   A low-water launch for *Norman Salvesen,* spring 1999, seen from the rocks to the east of the slipway.
(Tim Stevens)

23   47ft Tyne *Norman Salvesen* arrived at Sennen Cove in January 1999 to become the station's lifeboat.
Her first launch at Sennen took place on 23 January. (Tim Stevens)

24　Launch of 47ft Tyne *Norman Salvesen* at high water. (Peter Puddiphatt)

25　*Norman Salvesen* on the slipway during the opening ceremony of the refurbished lifeboat house, February 2002. (Nicholas Leach)

26   Sennen Cove lifeboat station 2002: 47ft Tyne *Norman Salvesen* and D Class inflatable *Spirit of the ACC* on the slipways outside the refurbished lifeboat house. (Nicholas Leach)

27   *Norman Salvesen* on the long slipway with relief 47ft Tyne *Voluntary Worker* (ON.1146) being hauled up the recovery slipway in February 2003. The relief boat was replacing *Norman Salvesen*, which left for refit and scheduled maintenance at DML, Plymouth. (Peter Puddiphatt)

The Four Boys approaches the RNLI Depot quayside, at Poole, during crew training before coming on station. (Phil Weeks)

The Four Boys on trials before coming to Sennen Cove. (By courtesy of the RNLI)

During their visit, the proud parents took a trip out on the lifeboat and presented to Anthony Oliver, the Institution's deputy head of fund-raising and marketing, a cheque for £7,600, the balance of their appeal which had raised a total of £97,000.

Between 18 and 22 November 1991 six of the lifeboat crew went to the RNLI Headquarters in Poole, for sea-training courses on their new lifeboat. Coxswain/Mechanic Terry George, Second Coxswain William Price, Assistant Mechanic Christopher Angove and crew members Philip Shannon, John Pender and Richard Manser were trained to operate the new boat and her equipment. The

lifeboat crew carried out various practical exercises as well as studying the lifeboat's construction and capabilities in the Training Centre at Poole. Emergency procedures, such as man overboard drill, fire fighting, and engine and steering failures were all practised, after which the lifeboat set off for her new station. She left at the end of the week and was sailed to Sennen under the command of John Unwin, RNLI Divisional Inspector of lifeboat for the South West. *The Four Boys* arrived at Sennen on 28 November 1991 to a tremendous welcome from the local community. As the first Mersey in the RNLI's fleet to be slipway launched, she went through several days of launching trials before being declared operational. On the day of the first launch, school children lined the beach to watch while a school of porpoises was on hand to observe proceedings. For the first launch, Coxswain/Mechanic George asked former Coxswain Maurice Hutchens to take the wheel, as the latter had been at the wheel of the lifeboat during the search for the four boys in 1985.

With the trials complete, *The Four Boys* was officially placed on station on 5 December 1991 and, on 22 April 1992, her formal naming and dedication ceremony was held. On hand to perform the christening was HRH the Duke of Kent who, eighteen years previously, had christened *Diana White*. The occasion was not only an important day in the history of the Sennen Cove station, but was also a day of memories for the parents and friends of the four schoolboys after whom the lifeboat was named. The Duke arrived promptly at 9.30 a.m. and was introduced to Coxswain/Mechanic Terry George and the lifeboat crew before taking his place on the platform. John Keeble then opened the proceedings by welcoming the Duke and all the assembled guests. Mrs Christine Ankers, mother of one of the drowned boys and representing the many donors, handed the lifeboat over to Michael Vernon, Chairman of the RNLI, who in turn placed the lifeboat into the care of the honorary secretary Captain James Summerlee. The service of dedication was conducted by Revd Dr R. Legg, rector of St Buryan, St Levan and Sennen, assisted by Revd H. Curnow, Methodist Minister for the St Just Circuit.

Arrival of *The Four Boys* at Sennen Cove on 28 November 1991. (Tony Denton)

Left above: The Four Boys on the slipway for the first time after her arrival at Sennen Cove on 28 November 1991. (Tony Denton)

Left middle: The Four Boys heads away from the slipway after her first launch, 28 November 1991. (Tony Denton)

Below: Recovery of *The Four Boys,* December 1991. She is hauled into the boathouse bow first up the short recovery slipway. (Tim Stevens)

After the dedication, the Duke was invited to name the lifeboat but, before doing so, he spoke of the background to the funding of the new boat, epitomising the feelings of those present:

> Sennen Cove now has a lifeboat to be proud of, and there are many people here today who will be sharing in that pride ... We have heard how the funding represents a combination of individual generosity, dedicated local support and a passion and desire for good to come out of tragedy. While this must be a happy day for you all, for the parents and families of Nicky Hurst, Jamie Holloway, Ricky Lamden and Robert Ankers, it will also bring bitter memories. You have shown great courage to confront your personal grief in such a positive and purposeful way. I can only assure you that in the Sennen Cove lifeboat crew you have the best possible men to ensure lives continue to be saved from these treacherous waters.

The Duke then named the lifeboat breaking the traditional champagne bottle across the bows of the new boat. After three cheers for the crew, he helped launch the boat by knocking out the pin connecting it to the winch wire. *The Four Boys* was put through her paces under the command of Coxswain Terry George, as a helicopter from RAF Culdrose flew above, streaming the RNLI flag. After the display, the Duke moved on to the Old Success Inn where he met the families of the crew and launchers, station and branch officials, the families of the boys and other guests. So ended a truly memorable day for Sennen Cove and its lifeboat station.

The 12m Mersey served at Sennen for seven years during which time she launched ninety times on service and is credited with saving forty-seven lives making her by far the busiest lifeboat at the station hitherto. The following descriptions encompass many of her rescues, the majority of which can be seen as somewhat routine in

The Four Boys is put through her paces at the end of her naming ceremony, 22 April 1992. (Tim Stevens)

The scene at the lifeboat house during the naming ceremony of *The Four Boys* on 22 April 1992. (Peter Puddiphatt)

nature, with greater detail provided about the most notable incidents in which she was involved. Her first full year on station, 1992, was a busy one. She launched on 3 January 1992 in south-westerly force six to gale-force eight winds with rough seas following reports of a person washed off the cliff at Pedn-men-du. However, after searching, nothing was found. Her first effective service took place on 10 May. She launched at 9.32 p.m. to assist the fishing vessel *Gorah Lass*, which was taking in water a mile north of Pendeen. The casualty was being towed by the St Ives lifeboat but was in danger of sinking and an escort was required as the light was failing. On 29 May at 2.56 p.m. *The Four Boys* launched to assist the capsized local fishing boat *Barry Anne* off the Longships. The lone fisherman on board had been very fortunate to be rescued by a passing yacht. The survivor was brought ashore by the lifeboat which also towed the submerged fishing boat back to the Cove where it was righted and hauled ashore.

During the afternoon of 23 June 1992, *The Four Boys* launched after the fishing vessel *Emblem* had been reported on fire five miles south-west of the Longships. The two crew from the casualty had been rescued by another fishing vessel and were transferred to the lifeboat and landed at Sennen. The lifeboat then returned to the scene and stood by while an attempt was made by HMS *Brecon* to extinguish the fire. *Emblem* was then taken in tow by the fishing vessel *Confide* only to sink shortly afterwards.

During the last ten days in July 1992 *The Four Boys* was called on five times to assist people in difficulty. On 21 July, she assisted to pump out the fishing boat *Sea Breeze*, which was taking in water two miles north-west of Pendeen. On 24 July she assisted the yacht *Skeabey-ny-Tonn* five miles north-west of the Longships after crab-pot

markers had fouled the yacht's propeller. The following day, she launched again to assist the diving inflatable *Raven II* which had capsized on Runnelstone Rock. The people clinging to the upturned hull in heavy swell were taken aboard the lifeboat while the vessel was righted and then towed to Penzance Harbour. All the survivors were safe and in good condition and so the lifeboat returned to station. On 28 July, *The Four Boys* assisted in a search for persons reported cut off by the tide at Porthcurno Bay and three days later she helped a small inflatable reported broken down eight miles west of Land's End. The inflatable's sole crew member was taken on board the lifeboat and the casualty towed back to Sennen Cove.

Between 19 August and 20 September 1992, the relief Mersey *Royal Shipwright* was on station while *The Four Boys* went for a routine overhaul. Although the relief lifeboat was called on a number of times, including searching for some missing divers on 29 August, none of the launches resulted in effective services and, in September, *The Four Boys* was back on station. On 26 September, the station lifeboat assisted in the recovery of an angler trapped by the tide on Aire Point, at the north end of Sennen Bay. On 3 November she helped the ketch *Lady Jazz*, which was disabled two miles south-west of Land's End, and towed the vessel to Newlyn. The final launch of the year took place on 2 December but after a search carried out in difficult conditions, nothing was found. As conditions prevented recovery at Sennen, the lifeboat proceeded to Newlyn and returned to Sennen the following day.

The following year, 1993, was a particularly busy one for the Sennen lifeboat. On 19 February, she assisted the fishing vessel *Children's Friend*, which had engine problems in the vicinity of the Runnelstone Buoy, and escorted her to Newlyn. On 4 March, she went to the sloop *El Animado* with an injured man aboard, ten miles south of Land's End. The injured man was airlifted to hospital by helicopter after initial treatment carried out by the lifeboat crew to make him more comfortable; the sloop was then towed to Newlyn.

The Four Boys tows the yacht *Nyota* into Newlyn Harbour, with St Michael's Mount in the background, on 16 May 1992. The lifeboat had launched at 1.20 p.m. to assist the yacht, which was disabled a mile west of Longships. (Peter Puddiphatt)

Recovery of *The Four Boys* up the
short slipway during lifeboat day,
26 July 1992. (Tim Stevens)

The Four Boys was involved in another tow on 16 May when she assisted the
French yacht *Ophelie*, reported to be disabled and lost ten miles north of Longships.
Two of the yacht's crew were taken on board the lifeboat and a tow was rigged. The
yacht was brought first to Sennen Cove, for shelter and then round Land's End and,
finally, on to the safety of Newlyn harbour. On 15 August, *The Four Boys* launched
at 9.48 p.m. to assist the fishing vessel *Alida T* which was on fire about eight miles
south of Porthcurno. The crew were rescued by another fishing vessel and the boat
taken in tow by Penlee lifeboat. The Sennen lifeboat extinguished the fire and
pumped out the vessel, then returned to station at 2 a.m. the following morning.
The 12m Mersey *Margaret Jean* (ON.1178), on relief duty in place of *The Four Boys*,
performed a long service on 15 September. She launched at 9.54 a.m. to assist the
yacht *La Madeleine*, of Pwllheli, which was disabled five miles west of Cape Cornwall,
without engine or steering. The lifeboat left the Cove at 9.54 a.m. and proceeded
on a VHF bearing directly to the casualty. After assessing the situation, the lifeboat
crew then embarked on a long tow to Newlyn, which was reached at 1.18 p.m. After
securing the yacht, the lifeboat returned to Sennen at 3.15 p.m. The final service of
the year took place on 10 December and involved another long tow, with *The Four
Boys* assisting the fishing vessel *Ben Loyal* which had engine failure to Newlyn.

Perhaps the most outstanding service undertaken by *The Four Boys* during her time
at Sennen took place on 6 December 1994. At 3.25 p.m. the Coastguard informed
the station that the fishing vessel *Julian Paul* (PZ.245) was in difficulty with a fouled

The Four Boys and RNAS helicopter 'Rescue 193' from 771 Squadron, RNAS Culdrose, exercise in the Bay for the benefit of visitors during the station's annual lifeboat day, 21 August 1994. Crew member Michael Tregear is being winched down to the lifeboat. (Tim Stevens)

propeller which the crew had been unable to free and requested that the lifeboat launch immediately. Five minutes later *The Four Boys,* under the command of Coxswain Terry George, put out in poor conditions with a force seven near-gale-force wind and choppy seas. The fishing vessel, owned by Harvey & Sons of Newlyn, was drifting in the spring flood tide four miles south-west of the Longships light. *The Four Boys* arrived on the scene at 3.55 p.m. after an uncomfortable passage during which the lifeboat pitched and rolled heavily. The casualty was a fully laden wood-hulled crabber lying across the weather and rolling heavily.

After discussing the options, the lifeboat crew passed a heaving line to the vessel and a tow was secured. By carefully applying power, Coxswain George took the strain and the lifeboat brought the casualty head to sea. The towline was then length-ened to 400m by using two lines and a buffer. The tow commenced at 4.05 p.m., heading south, but the lifeboat pitching heavily and shipping seas and spray overall, could make little headway against the tide. Although the tide would ease and turn in an hour, the forecast of worsening weather and the prospect of even worse wind-over-tide conditions led Coxswain George to request the assistance of Penlee lifeboat.

At 4.30pm, Penlee's 52ft Arun *Mabel Alice* (ON.1085) slipped her moorings and made best speed for Land's End in the force seven to eight gale. Meanwhile, Coxswain George established that the casualty had sufficient deck fittings to enable her to be towed by both lifeboats and he discussed his strategy with Penlee Coxswain Neil Brockman by radio. In very poor visibility, *Mabel Alice* found the two boats using her VHF-DF equipment and the searchlight shone by the Sennen lifeboat into the sky. Once on scene, another line was passed to the casualty by the Penlee lifeboat

crew demonstrating careful teamwork and taking advantage of the lifeboat's manoeuvrability. Once that line was secure, Coxswain Brockman took the strain. With both lifeboats towing together, progress was much easier and, by 6 p.m., the vessels were making three knots.

At 6.17 p.m. the line between the fishing vessel and *The Four Boys* parted and recovering the long line proved to be a time-consuming process. However, it became clear that the Penlee lifeboat was towing well on her own, so *The Four Boys* acted as an escort as the craft made for Newlyn harbour. Despite the fact that steady progress was made in the unpleasant conditions, the Sennen Cove lifeboat crew members were suffering from seasickness because of the need to keep the wheelhouse door shut in case of capsize. Meanwhile, *Mabel Alice* was continually being swept by spray and driving rain. At 10.30 p.m., a huge wave engulfed her and the lifeboatmen feared that the casualty would be swamped. The fishing vessel survived but the skipper was immediately instructed to get his crew into life-jackets and into the wheelhouse.

When Tater-Du was reached, the sea was estimated at 40ft and, although the motion had ceased, considerable skill was required to control the lifeboats at such slow speeds and in such big swells. At 12.14 a.m. on 7 December, Coxswain George took *The Four Boys* into Newlyn Harbour to check conditions at the entrance. At 12.37 a.m., Penlee lifeboat shortened the tow, while Sennen lifeboat stood by in case anything went wrong. Coxswain Brockman made for the south side of the entrance at best possible speed but, by the time the fishing vessel was through, two swells had pushed her up the north side. Despite this, she was safely inside and berthed alongside at 12.55 p.m. With the casualty secure, *The Four Boys* remained in Newlyn until the weather had improved sufficiently and she then returned to Sennen to rehouse after a difficult service.

For this outstanding service, Bronze medals were awarded to Coxswain George and to Penlee's Coxswain Brockman in recognition of 'fine seamanship, leadership and meritorious conduct' in very rough seas and storm-force winds. The medals were awarded in May 1995 by HRH the Duchess of Kent during the RNLI's Annual General Meeting and Presentation of Awards in London. Medal service certificates were presented to the Sennen crewmembers involved in the service: Second Coxswain John Pender, Assistant Mechanic Christopher Angove, John Jones, Daniel Shannon and Neil Willis. Willis was taking part in his very first all-weather rescue. The certificates were presented in November 1995, just under a year after the service, at a special ceremony at the Pirates Club, Penzance, by Captain Hugh Fogarty, Staff Officer at RNLI Headquarters, before a packed audience of well-wishers.

On 27 April 1995, the relief 12m Mersey *Lifetime Care* (ON.1148) was placed on station and remained until 18 September while *The Four Boys* went for some maintenance work. On 28 May, the relief lifeboat assisted the fishing vessel *Julian Paul*, which had engine trouble north-west of the Wolf Rock, and towed her to Newlyn. During August, *Lifetime Care* performed three rescues, the first on 2 August to the yacht *Klompen*, which was taking in water about four miles south-west of the Longships. A pump was put aboard the yacht which was then towed to Newlyn. Ten days later the relief lifeboat towed the powerboat *Buzzard*, anchored just off Cape Cornwall with engine failure, to Newlyn. *The Four Boys* returned to station in October and was called on three times during October and November for routine

Sennen Cove and Penlee lifeboatmen involved in the dramatic rescue of the Penzance-based fishing vessel *Julian Paul* in December 1994. Penlee Coxswain Neil Brockman is standing to the far right, with Sennen Cove Coxswain Terry George second right. Both Coxswains were awarded the RNLI's Bronze medal for their actions and leadership during the service. Left to right: -?- (Penlee), Graham Henderson (Penlee), -?- (Penlee), -?- (Penlee), -?- (Penlee), Mike Atkinson (Penlee), Martin Jones (Sennen Cove), Chris Angove (Sennen Cove), Neil Willis (Sennen Cove), John Pender (Second Coxswain, Sennen Cove), Daniel Shannon (Sennen Cove), Terry George (Coxswain, Sennen Cove), Neil Brockman (Coxswain, Penlee). (Tim Stevens)

Relief 12m Mersey *Lifetime Care* on exercise on 27 June 1995. The relief lifeboat stood in for *The Four Boys* between May and September 1995. (Tim Stevens)

services including, on 13 November, towing the small fishing boat *Fulmar*, in trouble off Porthcurno, to Newlyn.

December 1995 proved to be the busiest month of the year with *The Four Boys* launching five times. On 5 December she towed the fishing vessel *Taraqqi*, which had engine failure eleven miles north-west of the Sevenstones lightship, to Newlyn; the lifeboat returned at 1.45 a.m. the following day after a long service. On 15 December, she was called out in heavy snow showers, a north-easterly force seven to severe gale-force nine winds and rough seas after the cargo vessel *Arklow Bay* had suffered engine failure five miles south-west of Longships. The lifeboat launched at 8.16 p.m. and arrived on scene just over fifteen minutes later. A sister ship, *Arklow Marsh*, was in the vicinity and *The Four Boys* assisted in passing a tow from the casualty to the sister vessel. Both vessels were lying across the weather and rolling heavily, but *Arklow Marsh* commenced towing the vessel very slowly into the wind. The tow was taken over by the salvage tug *Kondor*, which had arrived at 12.30 a.m., and *Arklow Bay* was eventually taken to Falmouth. Whilst returning to station from assisting *Arklow Bay*, *The Four Boys* was diverted at 2.05 a.m. on 16 December to assist the fishing vessel *Cheryl Elizabeth*. The vessel was escorted to Newlyn and pumped out; the lifeboat returned to Sennen at 7.45 a.m. Finally, on 19 December, the fishing vessel *Superb*, broken down to the west of Wolf Rock, was towed to Newlyn and the following day *The Four Boys* launched at 2.08 p.m. to recover a life raft spotted off Pendeen, ending a busy year for the lifeboat and her crew.

During June 1996, *The Four Boys* was called out four times to assist small motor vessels. On 11 June she went to the Sennen fishing vessel *Barry Ann*, but was not required and, the following day, launched at 8.35 p.m. to assist the fishing vessel *Jackie G*,

Recovery of *The Four Boys* after a routine exercise. (Tim Stevens)

which had engine failure and was taking in water two miles south–east of Wolf Rock. The vessel was towed to Newlyn and the lifeboat returned to station at 1.35 a.m. the following day. On 27 June, she assisted the motor boat *Barbary T* which had broken down off Gwennap Head and, two days later, went to assist the motor yacht *Zarzuela*. The yacht's engine had failed in a position four miles south–east of Wolf Rock and her crew were suffering from seasickness. The yacht was towed to Newlyn Harbour. Further routine services followed with *The Four Boys* assisting the fishing vessel *Scarlet Thread* with a fouled propeller north–west of the Longships in the early hours of 24 August 1996 while, on 17 December, she helped the fishing vessel *Rebecca Elaine*, which had engine failure five miles south–south–west of Gwennap Head.

The Four Boys launched to a wide variety of casualties in 1997, starting on 19 February with the cargo vessel *Innisfree*, which had broken down and was drifting towards the shore about three miles south–west of the Longships in a westerly force six to severe gale-force nine wind and rough sea. The vessel restarted her engine without needing any assistance and proceeded on passage, but the lifeboat had to shelter in Newlyn overnight and returned to station following day. On 11 March, *The Four Boys* was involved in a long search for survivors from the St Ives fishing vessel *Gorah Lass*, which had foundered to the north–east of St Ives. Lifeboats from St Ives, Newquay and Padstow were involved as well as a helicopter from RNAS Culdrose. The search ended in tragedy when two persons were recovered by the St Ives lifeboat but were pronounced dead on arrival at hospital, while the third crew member was never found.

On 29 June 1997, *The Four Boys* worked with the station's inshore lifeboat following receipt by the Coastguard of satellite distress signals from the Land's End

The Four Boys on exercise off Land's End. (Peter Puddiphatt)

The Four Boys is pulled up the slipway bow first during recovery, 28 July 1996. The boat was recovered bow first until hydraulics were fitted to the turntable in anticipation of the arrival of a 47ft Tyne to replace the Mersey. *The Four Boys* was therefore the last lifeboat to be recovered in this way, a practice that had been introduced almost seventy years before. (Tim Stevens)

The Four Boys on the slipway in July 1996 while alterations were made to the lifeboat house in readiness for a 47ft Tyne. (Paul Richards)

vicinity. Immediately after launching at 4.05 a.m., a red flare was spotted from the shore near Nanquidno and the yacht *Boucanier* was found hard aground. The ILB was then requested and was able to rescue the yacht's only occupant. The yacht was subsequently refloated by the lifeboat and towed to Newlyn. Later the same day, *The Four Boys* went to the assistance of the fishing vessel *Virgo Lady*, which had broken down near Wolf Rock. On 26 July and 3 August the lifeboat assisted yachts *Charisma* and *Rip Rap* respectively and towed both to Newlyn. On 12 September she launched at 6.55 p.m. to assist two injured men on the cargo vessel *Heinrich Bojen*, which was five miles south-west of the Wolf Rock. The two seamen had been overcome by fumes and were airlifted to hospital, but the rest of the crew were fine so the vessel continued on her way and the lifeboat returned to station.

During 1998, *The Four Boys* undertook three effective services, all routine in nature, which were going to be the last rescues she carried out as the Sennen lifeboat. The first took place on 3 July to the fishing vessel *Catherine* which had engine failure in the vicinity of Wolf Rock. The lifeboat launched at 2.20 p.m. and towed the casualty to Newlyn Harbour. On 12 August *The Four Boys* towed the converted fishing vessel *Feasible* to Penzance. The vessel was in need of assistance after engine failure four miles west of Cape Cornwall. What proved to be the last service by *The Four Boys* took place on 24 September. She launched at 9.20 p.m. to the fishing vessel *Tir-Na-Nag*, which had been reported overdue from a fishing trip out of Hayle. A search was carried out with the St Ives lifeboat and inshore lifeboat, Padstow lifeboat and a rescue helicopter. The casualty was eventually located by *The Four Boys*, using radar, twelve miles north of Gurnard's Head. The lone occupant was safe and so the vessel was taken in tow. The tow was passed to the St Ives lifeboat which returned the casualty to Hayle.

The Four Boys on exercise just off the slipway. (Peter Puddiphatt)

The Four Boys assists to refloat the single-handed yacht *Boucanier* ashore at PolPry, near Nanquidno, on 29 June 1997, with D Class inflatable D-490 standing by. (Peter Puddiphatt)

Above: The Four Boys launching during filming for the Air-Sea Rescue Show at the Land's End Complex. A cameraman was strapped to the radar mast filming the launch, Spring 1998. (Tim Stevens)

In 1997, a decision was made to improve lifeboat cover at Land's End and station a 47ft Tyne class lifeboat at Sennen Cove. The new lifeboat was longer, faster and heavier than the 12m Mersey and was specifically designed for slipway launching. A larger, heavier and more powerful boat was considered to be better suited to the sea conditions off Land's End and better able to perform the kind of services that the Sennen lifeboat was undertaking. It was possible to station a 47ft Tyne at Sennen after dredging the channel off the slipway had been successfully completed. After her last service in September 1998, *The Four Boys* remained on station until December 1998,

Opposite below: The Four Boys launching for Penberth Cove lifeboat day on 19 July 1998. Note that the radar mast is still folded down as she was launched from inside the boathouse. (Tim Stevens)

Right: The Four Boys on exercise at Penberth Cove, 19 July 1998. (Tim Stevens)

Below: The Four Boys on exercise at Pendeen in April 1998 with D-490 *Spirit of the ACC.* (Tim Stevens)

spending the last few weeks of her time at Sennen outside the boathouse, at the head of the long slipway, while modifications were made to the launching arrangements in preparation for the Tyne.

Following her final launch on the morning of 5 December, *The Four Boys* was placed on her mooring while slipway trials took place with the Tyne class lifeboat. While on her mooring a rainbow formed in the wintery sky with one end directly above the lifeboat. The sight of a lifeboat resembling the legendary pot of gold represented a very poignant moment for onlookers on what proved to be the last day for

The Four Boys at the RNLI Depot, Poole, on 17 February 1999 shortly after being replaced as station lifeboat at Sennen Cove. (Nicholas Leach)

The Four Boys at Sennen Cove. She was well thought of by all the Sennen crew, particularly because of the source of her funding, and she was a great servant of the station. After leaving Sennen, *The Four Boys* was taken to the RNLI Depot, at Poole, and then transferred to a boatyard to be overhauled and painted in the RNLI's new corporate livery. She then represented the Institution at its 175th Anniversary celebrations at Poole in June 1999, forming part of the Lifeboat Flotilla which sailed past Poole Quay on 23 June. By this time she had been allocated to her new station, Amble in Northumberland, and, after training for the Amble crew between 28 June and 2 July 1999 had been completed, she was sailed north up the east coast to her new station. She was placed on station at Amble on 22 July 1999.

Norman Salvesen

The 'new' lifeboat for Sennen was the 47ft Tyne *Norman Salvesen* which had in fact been built in 1988 for the Wick station in northern Scotland. Provided from the bequest of the late Mrs Mary 'Mickie' Salvesen, she was placed on station at Wick in September 1988. She had initially been slipway launched but in 1994 was placed on a sheltered mooring afloat in Wick Harbour after a new berth had been found for her there. When a new lifeboat was sent to Wick in February 1997, *Norman Salvesen* was available for reallocation, having launched on service 120 times and saved fifty-four lives during her time in Scotland, and it was then announced she was to go to Sennen.

The 47ft Tyne class lifeboat was developed during the 1980s – before the 12m Mersey – as a slipway-launched lifeboat with double the speed of the traditional double-ended displacement lifeboats she was to replace at stations throughout the

British Isles. The boat had a semi-planing hull constructed from steel, with a shallow draught, long straight keel and extended bilge keels to protect the propellers, features necessary for slipway launching as well as working in shoal waters. The wide keel ended in a hauling shoe which was used for winching the boat back into its house. The hull shape of the new design enabled a top speed of approximately eighteen knots to be achieved by the twin propellers each being driven by a 425hp General Motors 6V-92-TI diesel engine. Before *Norman Salvesen* came to Sennen, she was re-engined with more powerful twin General Motors 6V-92TA D-DEC diesel engines, each developing 525hp giving her a slightly increased speed. Data about the computer-managed engines are displayed on twin screens in the wheelhouse. The engines draw fuel from two main tanks which hold 510 gallons of diesel between them, with a reserve tank of 102 gallons, giving a range at full speed of 238 nautical miles. The boat is self-righting by virtue of the inherent buoyancy in the super-structure, combined with the weight of the engines positioned in the boat to lower the centre of gravity. Seated accommodation in the wheelhouse is provided for a crew of six, with an additional 'jumper' seat for a doctor.

In place of *The Four Boys* in December 1998 came the relief 47ft Tyne class lifeboat *Mariners Friend* (ON.1142) which remained on duty until 21 January 1999. The relief boat was needed because, during the passage to her new station, *Norman Salvesen* suffered minor problems with her engines and had to be taken to Falmouth for repairs to be carried out. She did not arrive at Sennen until January 1999 despite being officially placed 'on service' in December 1998. The new lifeboat was formally

47ft Tyne *Norman Salvesen* moored in Wick harbour in July 1995. She served at Wick for almost a decade before coming to Sennen. During her time at the Scottish station she launched 120 times on service and saved fifty-four lives. (Nicholas Leach)

After serving at
Wick and having
been reallocated
to Sennen,
Norman Salvesen
was taken to
Souter's Shipyard
at Cowes to be
overhauled and
repainted ready
for her new
station.
(Peter Edey)

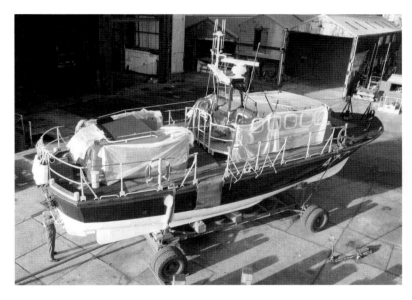

Norman Salvesen
at Souter's
Shipyard, Cowes,
in 1998 after
being refitted for
Sennen.
(Peter Edey)

Opposite above: With her newly-painted hull glistening, *Norman Salvesen* is lifted into the water at Souter's Shipyard, Cowes, after her refit in 1998. (Peter Edey)

Opposite middle: Norman Salvesen in the water at Souter's Shipyard, Cowes, after her refit and is ready for service at Sennen Cove. (Peter Edey)

Opposite below: Before *Norman Salvesen* was placed on station at Sennen, the lifeboat crew spent time familiarizing themselves with and exercising on the craft. She was at Fowey in December 1998 with the windows covered so that navigation using radar and instruments alone could be practised by the crew. (Paul Richards)

The first 47ft Tyne to serve at Sennen Cove was the relief lifeboat *Mariners Friend* (ON.1142) which arrived at the station on 5 December 1998. She replaced 12m Mersey *The Four Boys*, which launched to meet her, accompanied by D Class inflatable *Spirit of the ACC*. (Tim Stevens)

This photograph shows the recovery of 47ft Tyne *Norman Salvesen* at Sennen on 23 January 1999 after her first launch as station lifeboat. (John Chappell)

rededicated at a ceremony held on 29 June 1999 at the Harbour Beach. She was handed over by Air Vice Marshal John Tetley, CB, a vice president of the RNLI, into the care of the station and accepted by John Chappell, the station's honorary secretary. The Service of Dedication was conducted by Revd Harry Burlton, Rector of St Buryan, St Sennen and St Levan, and a vote of thanks was proposed by Lt John Unwin at the end of the ceremony.

The first service performed by *Norman Salvesen* at Sennen took place on 25 March 1999, before her formal rededication. She launched at 10.35 p.m. to evacuate an ill man from the tug *Christine*, three miles north-west of Land's End and arrived on scene at 10.50 p.m. Rescue helicopter Rescue 193 had been on the scene for some time but was having difficulty winching the patient off the tug due to the tug's high masts. The lifeboat stood by until, at approximately 11.30 p.m., the helicopter succeeded in recovering the casualty and took him to Treliske Hospital, Truro. *Norman Salvesen* returned to station at midnight and rehoused in a moderate to rough sea.

After this first service, *Norman Salvesen* went on to have a busy first year at her new station. In May, she assisted the yacht *Skyla B* and towed her to Newlyn Harbour while, later the same month, provided similar assistance to the fishing vessel *Scarlet Thread* which had suffered engine trouble six miles north-west of Sennen Cove. During July, *Norman Salvesen* assisted three motor vessels which had got into difficulty and on 26 of the month assisted the yacht *Sirenia* which was making heavy weather about three miles north-west of the Wolf Rock. The yacht was escorted to a safe mooring at Sennen Cove in an easterly force five to seven wind and moderate to rough sea. During this service the lifeboat sustained some damage just after launching and, once the service was completed, she proceeded to Falmouth on one engine for repairs. In her place, two days later, came the relief lifeboat *The Famous Grouse*. The relief boat stayed at Sennen until 20 August 1999 during which time she performed just one rescue, on 6 August 1999, helping the yacht *Callianeira* which had a fouled propeller and rudder and was anchored seven miles north-west of Pendeen Lighthouse. The yacht was towed to Newlyn and the lifeboat returned to Sennen Cove at 2.30 p.m.

By the end of August 1999 *Norman Salvesen* was back on station and, on 26 August, she was launched to assist in recovering the Sennen Cove fishing boat *Boy Matt*, which had been swamped a mile south-west of the Brisons. The two crew had been rescued by helicopter after almost two and a half hours clinging to their boat. The submerged fishing boat was towed back to Sennen Cove, righted with the aid of the inshore lifeboat and returned to the harbour. On 18 September *Norman Salvesen* was involved in a fairly long service. She launched at 5.38 p.m. to assist the yacht *Marisol*, with five persons on board, which was disabled seventeen miles north-west of Sennen Cove. Once the lifeboat arrived at the scene, the yacht was taken in tow and both boats made for Newlyn. They arrived at 1 a.m. on 19 September but the lifeboat remained in the harbour to await an improvement in sea conditions at Sennen as the service had been undertaken in southerly force six to eight winds and rough seas. She was eventually recovered at 1 p.m., twelve hours after arriving at Newlyn.

During 2000, two relief 47ft Tyne lifeboats were temporarily on station, the first of which, *The Famous Grouse* (ON.1133), arrived on 21 January when *Norman Salvesen* left for routine maintenance work. This relief lifeboat launched on

The scene at Sennen during the rededication of *Norman Salvesen* on 29 June 1999 at the Harbour Beach by the Revd Harry Burlton, Rector of St Buryan, St Sennen and St Levan. The lifeboat crew line the slipway in front of the lifeboat. (Paul Richards)

Norman Salvesen at sea after her rededication service, approaching the harbour. (Paul Richards)

Recovery of *Norman Salvesen* up the short slipway after the service of rededication, June 1999. The three standing on the slipway, to left, are from left to right Frank Smith (Coxswain, Salcombe lifeboat), Keith Stuart (Coxswain, Fowey lifeboat) and Dan Atkinson (crew member, Humber lifeboat). (Paul Richards)

24 February at 7.04 p.m. to assist the fishing vessel *Harvest Reaper* with two persons on board. The vessel, which was taking in water in heavy weather two miles southwest of the Longships lighthouse, was escorted to Newlyn Harbour and pumped out. Three days later *The Famous Grouse* launched during the late evening to assist the veteran tank-landing craft *Rhino*, which was experiencing steering difficulties six miles west of Pendeen lighthouse, with four persons on board. The vessel was escorted round Land's End and part way across Mount's Bay. On 14 April, the second of the relief 47ft Tynes, *Voluntary Worker* (ON.1146), arrived at the station. She launched at 7.10 a.m. on 30 April to the yacht *Mercurial Spirit*, with four persons on board, which had suffered a broken rudder three miles southwest of The Runnelstone. The yacht was towed to Newlyn Harbour and the relief lifeboat returned to Sennen Cove at 11.30 p.m.

On 16 May 2000, *Norman Salvesen* returned to her station and, on 29 May, she launched to assist the yacht *Mouflon*, with four persons on board, which had a fouled propeller and so was towed to Newlyn Harbour. The summer was quiet and the lifeboat was not needed again until 30 November when she launched at 5.15 p.m. to assist the fishing vessel *Intuition*, with four persons on board, which had gearbox failure four miles south of Longships and was drifting towards the shore in severe gale-force winds. By the time the lifeboat arrived on scene at about 5.50 p.m., the vessel had regained some power and was proceeding to Newlyn at slow speed so *Norman Salvesen* escorted the vessel as far as Sennen harbour through very rough seas. But as the short recovery slipway was obstructed by scaffolding and in view of the prevailing conditions, the lifeboat remained at Newlyn overnight and was rehoused at 8 a.m. the following day, once the scaffolding had been removed by the contractors.

The 47ft Tyne was the first lifeboat at Sennen to be restricted to stern-first recovery as her predecessors were brought up the slipway bow first and turned on the turntable at the head of the slipway. These two photographs show *Norman Salvesen* being recovered on 25 May 1999 with Coxswain Terry George at the helm. She approaches the breakwater to attach a line which is used to veer back onto the short slipway. With her stern on the toe of the short slipway, two breasting ropes are passed to the lifeboat and taken down both sides of the boat to prevent bow movement during the recovery sequence. (Tim Stevens)

On 3 October 2000, Sennen Cove lifeboat took part in Exercise Kernow, a major exercise involving maritime rescue services in Cornwall. The scenario for the exercise was that the Penzance to Isles of Scilly passenger-ferry *Scillonian III* had been in collision with the motor tanker *Amity*, suffered a major engine fire and was adrift and powerless with several casualties aboard. The exercise was carried out in two phases: the first was a search and rescue operation followed by anti–pollution procedures. *Norman Salvesen* launched and stood by the ferry with the Lizard lifeboat *David Robinson* (ON.1145) and Penlee lifeboat *Mabel Alice* (ON.1085). Due to force

seven to eight winds and poor sea conditions, the transfer of casualties from the ferry to lifeboats was deemed too dangerous and any vessel going alongside the 'casualty' would have suffered damage too, an unnecessary risk for what was only an exercise. Helicopters from RNAS Culdrose were successful in winching a team of fire-fighters from Cornwall Fire Brigade's Falmouth station aboard the ferry to fight the fire and the Coastguard ETV *Far Sky* stood by to take *Scillonian* in tow. Three hours after arriving on scene, the lifeboats were stood down and then returned to their respective stations.

During December 2000, *Norman Salvesen* was involved in helping two large vessels. On 2 December, she launched at 3.40 p.m. to take over escort duties from St Ives lifeboat for the 110ft beam trawler *Silver Harvester,* of Penzance, which had lost steering early in the morning when approximately thirty miles north-west of Trevose Head. The Padstow lifeboat *James Burrough* (ON.1094) had initially gone to her aid, followed by St Ives lifeboat. Both lifeboats had spent several hours towing the vessel towards St Ives Bay. Once the crew of *Silver Harvester* had managed to jury-rig the vessel's steering system to give them some control, it was decided to head for Newlyn with the vessel under her own power. Sennen Cove lifeboat met up with the two boats about five miles north-west of Pendeen and the St Ives lifeboat then returned to station after six hours at sea. *Norman Salvesen* then escorted *Silver Harvester* round Land's End in a moderate sea and into Newlyn, arriving at 7.30 p.m.

On 21 December, *Norman Salvesen* went to the aid of the cargo vessel *Jens R*, with six persons on board, which had suffered engine failure approximately four miles south-east of the Runnelstone. The Coastguard Emergency Towing Vessel (ETV) *Far*

Relief 47ft Tyne *The Famous Grouse* on a routine exercise off Sennen Cove in April 2000. She served for a couple of months during early 2000 while *Norman Salvesen* was away for maintenance work. (Peter Edey)

Left above: Norman Salvesen on exercise, 2001. (Tim Stevens)

Left middle: Norman Salvesen is launched in July 2001 to go to Penberth for that village's local lifeboat day. (Nicholas Leach)

Below: Norman Salvesen arriving at Penberth in July 2001 for the local lifeboat day. (Nicholas Leach)

Sky had been sent from Falmouth when the incident started earlier in the day. By the time the lifeboat arrived on scene at 10.50 a.m., the tug was already in attendance and the vessel was just over two miles from the shore with a probable grounding area around Porthgwarra. *Far Sky* was able to take *Jens R* in tow and set course for Falmouth with the lifeboat escorting the vessels for a short time until they were well clear of the land. *Norman Salvesen* returned to Sennen at 12.45 p.m.

Between 29 December 2000 and 1 March 2001, the relief 47ft Tyne *City of Sheffield* (ON.1131) was on station in place of *Norman Salvesen*. She performed only one service, on 25 January, to assist the fishing vessel *Vagabond* with five persons on board which had suffered total engine failure near Sevenstones Lightvessel. The casualty was towed to Newlyn in moderate to rough seas.

Just over a month after returning to station, *Norman Salvesen* launched on 6 April 2001 at 3.30 p.m. to assist the dismasted French yacht *Saturnin* which was in difficulty in severe gale-force nine winds and rough seas about four miles west–north-west of Pendeen. Half an hour after launching, the lifeboat reached the casualty which had only one person on board. He remained on board his vessel as a tow was established and after an uncomfortable passage, both lifeboat and yacht arrived at Newlyn at 7.30 p.m. Due to deteriorating conditions, the lifeboat was forced to remain at Newlyn until the morning of 8 April.

A month later, on 6 May 2001, *Norman Salvesen* launched to assist the 25ft motor boat *Our Louise* with two persons on board, towing her to Newlyn. At 5.20 a.m. on 24 June, the lifeboat was launched to assist the yacht *Questor* with two persons on board. The yacht had left Newport, Rhode Island, on 21 May and had run low on fuel and food during her transatlantic crossing. She was disabled in calm conditions and so the lifeboat towed her to Newlyn. Five days later, on 29 June, *Norman Salvesen*

The refurbished lifeboat house with 47ft Tyne *Norman Salvesen* and D Class inflatable D-490 on the slipways. (Nicholas Leach)

Left above: 47ft Tyne *Norman Salvesen* on the slipway for the formal opening and dedication of the refurbished lifeboat house, February 2002. (Nicholas Leach)

Left below: Coxswain Terry George receives a framed print of *Susan Ashley* off the Longships lighthouse during the formal opening ceremony of the refurbished lifeboat house, February 2002. (Nicholas Leach)

launched during the late evening to assist another sailing vessel, the 58ft ketch *Schiehallion*, with two persons on board. The yacht had struck the bottom whilst passing between the Brisons and Cape Cornwall and sought a safe anchorage in Sennen Bay to assess any damage. After consultation with the Coastguard, it was decided to tow the vessel to Newlyn Harbour. On 30 September, *Norman Salvesen* performed a difficult service in southerly strong to gale-force winds. She launched at 1.25 a.m. to assist the Newlyn fishing vessel *Vagabond*, with five persons on board, which had engine failure three miles west of Longships. With the weather deterio-rating, a tow was rigged and the vessel was taken to Newlyn where both boats arrived at 5.15 a.m. The lifeboat then returned to Sennen at 8.30 a.m. and was rehoused.

During the early hours of 20 April 2002, *Norman Salvesen* launched to assist the cargo vessel *Emma Pline*, with six persons on board, which had suffered engine failure and was drifting towards the shore three miles south of Gwennap Head in a severe gale-force nine wind, gusting to 65 mph, and rough sea. The Coastguard's Emergency Towing Vessel *Anglian Prince* also proceeded to the scene but engineers on board the

cargo vessel repaired her engine and she continued on passage at 3.45 a.m. The lifeboat proceeded to Newlyn as severe weather at Sennen prevented recovery.

In June 2002, the relief lifeboat *Owen and Anne Aisher* (ON.1122) was on station when an urgent request was received from the Coastguard at Falmouth to assist the fishing vessel *Stereden Va Bro*, which had reported an engine room fire, near the Runnelstone, on 8 June. Speed of launch is usually important when launching the lifeboat but was particularly important in this instance and so the lifeboat left the Cove at 7.14 a.m. with a minimal crew due to the urgency of the situation. She arrived on scene at 7.32 a.m. and, although no obvious sign of fire could be seen, the crew reported the bulkhead was very hot so three crew members were taken off. The skipper was left on board to tend the line as the lifeboat set course for Newlyn with the casualty in tow. Then, at about 8 a.m., smoke was observed coming from the wheelhouse, so the tow was immediately cast off by the lifeboatmen and the lifeboat went alongside to take the skipper off. Within five minutes of the first sign of smoke, the whole of the fishing vessel's wheelhouse and accommodation was engulfed in flames. *Owen and Anne Aisher* remained in the area until the Penlee lifeboat *Mabel Alice* (ON.1085) arrived and then she proceeded to Newlyn where the survivors were landed. She then returned to the scene, stood by with *Mabel Alice* until the Coastguard ETV *Anglian Prince* arrived on scene and then returned to Sennen where she arrived at midday.

During December 2002 *Norman Salvesen* was called out on consecutive days to vessels that had got into difficulty in strong easterly winds and moderate to rough seas. On 9 December she launched at 2.15 p.m. to stand by the German coaster *Hikie*

Norman Salvesen is launched in summer 2002 with the Sea Core Rig moored in the channel ready for dredging work to improve accessibility for the lifeboat. (Tim Stevens)

which had broken down with machinery failure six miles west of the Longships and arrived on scene at 2.50 p.m. Concern was expressed by the Coastguard that she might drift onto Sevenstones so, together with St Mary's lifeboat *The Whiteheads* (ON.1229), she stood by the vessel until she had drifted safely clear. *Norman Salvesen* was released at 6.15 p.m. by when the Coastguard ETV *Anglian Prince* was on its way and took the ship in tow to Falmouth. The following day, she put out at 7 a.m. to assist the yacht *Mercurial Spirit*, with two persons on board, which had torn sails near the Wolf Rock and was unable to make headway. The lifeboat reached the yacht at 7.42 a.m. and took it in tow. During the passage to Newlyn, speed was kept to a minimum to avoid damage to the light yacht which had no substantial towing point. The safety of Newlyn Harbour was reached at midday and the casualty was berthed enabling the lifeboat to return to station.

In 2003, the 150th anniversary of the founding of the station was celebrated. To commemorate this milestone, HRH the Duke of Kent, President of the RNLI, visited the station on 9 May 2003 to present a Vellum. Greeted by the children of Sennen School on his arrival, the Duke was then introduced to local dignitaries before touring the lifeboat station and souvenir shop. He met the crew, shore crew, Station Committee and Guild before presenting the Vellum to Second Coxswain Philip Shannon, a member of the crew for thirty-seven years. The Duke was presented with a framed picture of the Sennen Cove lifeboat before retiring for a cup of tea and a chat with, amongst others, retired Coxswain Maurice Hutchens. During the anniversary year both of the station's lifeboats were away for refits: *Norman Salvesen* was at DML, Devonport, for a full five-yearly refit with relief Tyne *Voluntary Worker* (ON.1146) in her place. The inshore lifeboat D-490 *Spirit of the ACC* was also taken away for a routine refit with a relief D Class inflatable D-459 *Margaret and Fiona Wood* on station in her place.

Left: Second Coxswain Philip Shannon with the 150th anniversary vellum. (Tim Stevens)

Right: HRH the Duke of Kent at Sennen Cove lifeboat stations during the presentation of the 150th anniversary vellum. (Zara Thomas, by courtesy of Tim Stevens)

Right: Nan Bearson, the first female crew member at Sennen Cove, joined the crew in 1999. (Tim Stevens)

Middle: 47ft Tyne *Norman Salvesen* on the long slipway about to depart for refit and overhaul at DML, Devonport, February 2003. (Peter Puddiphatt)

Bottom: With *Norman Salvesen* on the long slipway, relief 47ft Tyne *Voluntary Worker* (ON.1146) is brought into the harbour ready for recovery up the short slipway, February 2003. (Peter Puddiphatt)

At the end of March 2003, relief lifeboat *Voluntary Worker* and the lifeboat crew had a busy few days. On 22 March the lifeboat was called into action after the German cargo ship RMS *Mülheim* ran aground at 4.30 a.m. near Pedn-men-du, between Sennen Cove and Land's End. The lifeboat was launched, accompanied by the D Class ILB, with the Land's End cliff team and a rescue helicopter from RNAS Culdrose also on hand. The ship had six crew on board, five of whom were taken off by the rescue helicopter and brought to the lifeboat station where they were met by ambulance staff to be treated for shock before going to the Seaman's Mission at Newlyn. The master remained on board the 1,846grt Antigua & Barbados registered vessel, which was carrying a cargo of scrap from Cork to Lübeck when she hit the rocks. The Coastguard Emergency Towing Vessel *Far Sky* proceeded to the area at 9 a.m. and the tug *Neftegaz 57* was also on scene with the helicopter ready to evacuate the master.

On 25 March, *Voluntary Worker* launched at 11.30 a.m. to assist the Newlyn fishing vessel *Little Waters*, which was three miles south-west of the Runnelstone with a fouled propeller. On 27 March she assisted a single-handed racing yacht dismasted seven miles south-east of the Runnelstone. Two lifeboat crew went aboard the yacht to help stow the broken rigging and the vessel was taken to Newlyn. The following day, both Sennen lifeboats again went to the cargo vessel RMS *Mülheim*, after four salvage workers had become trapped on the wreck in the fog. The men were taken off the ship by the ILB, transferred to the ALB and both boats returned to Sennen at 4 p.m. Fears were expressed locally that the cargo vessel would cause an environmental

The German cargo vessel RMS *Mülheim* aground at Castle Zawn, Gamper Bay, Land's End, on 22 March 2003. Rescue helicopter 193 or 771 Squadron at RNAS Culdrose air-lifts the vessel's Captain at 7 a.m. with both Sennen Cove lifeboats in attendance. (Ollie George, by courtesy of Tim Stevens)

Washed by the breaking surf, RMS *Mülheim* on the rocks on 22 March 2003, the morning after she went ashore. (Tim Stevens)

Relief lifeboat Voluntary Worker stands by RMS *Mülheim* on 22 March 2003 at 6.30 a.m., just before the rescue helicopter lifted her Captain off. (Ollie George, courtesy of Tim Stevens)

disaster and some pollutants and debris were washed up on beaches in the vicinity. Dutch salvage experts stated that the cargo vessel could not be brought off the rocks but would have to be broken up after the pollutants had been removed. The vessel was gradually dismantled where she lay and, by the end of May 2003, salvage operations had been concluded.

The inshore lifeboat

Although the inshore lifeboat (ILB) has been in service with the RNLI since the early 1960s, an inshore craft based at Sennen Cove to cover Whitesand Bay and the beaches around Land's End was not deemed necessary until the 1990s. However, by the early 1990s, a requirement for an ILB in the area was identified during one of the RNLI's regular reviews of the coast. The decision to extend lifeboat cover was made as a result of the number of search and rescue incidents occurring within the capabilities of an ILB. The ILB, known as the D Class inflatable, is the smallest lifeboat in the RNLI fleet. Since being introduced in 1963, the design has been refined and developed and the craft has become an efficient, effective and essential life-saving tool. The 16ft inflatable lifeboats, made from tough nylon coated with hypalon, are usually crewed by two or three, powered by a 40hp outboard engine and can be launched quickly and easily. They are equipped with VHF radio, GPS, flexible fuel tanks, flares, an anchor, a spare propeller, a compass, first aid kit and knife. The ILB's advantage over the conventional lifeboat was its speed which, at

twenty knots, was considerably faster than any lifeboat in service during the 1960s, as well as its ease of launching. The ILB also has the advantage of being able to go alongside other craft easily, or pick up persons in the water, without causing or suffering damage.

The first inshore lifeboat to be sent to Sennen was D-365, built in 1988 to serve in the Relief Fleet. She arrived on 22 February 1994 for evaluation trials and stayed until 29 March. On 29 March, she was replaced by D-450 *Anthony*, another relief ILB, which stayed until 9 November 1994 and during the summer the D Class inflatable proved its worth. D-450 was first called into action on 21 May 1994 to investigate a small boat thought to be in trouble near Nanquidno, but after the lifeboat crew found all was well and the ILB's services were not required she returned to station. She was called out again the following day after clothing had been found on Gwenver beach but, since no swimmers could be found, she returned to station without being needed.

The ILB's first effective service took place on 18 June 1994 when she went to investigate a small boat thought to be in trouble near Gwennap Head and recovered an abandoned 8ft skiff. Three days later she assisted the Penwith Council rescue boat which had broken down in deteriorating weather and also escorted a canoe to safety. During August, the ILB was called upon five times and carried out a number of routine services including searching for missing divers and swimmers and investigating a becalmed yacht. On 9 August, D-450 was launched at 5.55 p.m. to assist *The Four Boys* and bring ashore two persons from the yacht *Sterelen Mor* which was being towed into the Cove by the all-weather lifeboat. By September 1994, the ILB at Sennen had been launched twelve times on service and, in an official report, Captain Hugh Fogarty, Divisional Inspector of Lifeboats for the south, confirmed: 'There is a need for inshore lifeboat cover at Sennen Cove.' The ILB was therefore established permanently, on a summer-only basis initially, after successfully coming through the year of evaluation.

One of the first D Class inflatable ILBs to serve at Sennen was D-450 *Anthony*, which served on temporary station duty. She is pictured here being launched on exercise in April 1994. (Tim Stevens)

For the 1995 season, D-448 *Sea Ranger*, another relief inshore lifeboat, was sent to the station. She arrived on 30 March, remained until 8 November and performed six launches during her time at the Cove. During April she performed three services, the third of which came while she was on exercise. At 4.20 p.m. she was diverted to investigate a report of a fallen climber at Bosigran. The climber was evacuated to hospital by helicopter and the ILB returned to station. After a launch on 2 May when her services were not required, she was not called upon again until October. On 5 and 25 of that month she launched to investigate reports that people were in danger, but on both occasions found that her services were not required.

For the 1996 season, the station operated a new D Class inflatable, D-490, which was to be the station's own ILB. This boat arrived on 28 February and, two days later, was officially placed on station. The ILB was one of five provided by Officers and Soldiers of The Royal Logistic Corps with contributions from The Regimental Association, The Royal Engineers and The Trustees of The Royal Logistics Corps. The other ILBs funded by The Royal Logistic Corps were stationed at St Ives, Port Issac, Torbay and Looe. The new ILB was formally named *Spirit of the ACC* and dedicated at a ceremony on 30 June 1996 at the Harbour Beach. The ILB was handed over to the RNLI by Colonel Tony Barnett, OBE, Colonel Commandant, The Royal Logistic Corps, and accepted by Air Vice Marshal John Tetley, CB, CVO, on behalf of the RNLI. Dr Richard Manser, honorary secretary of the Sennen Cove Branch, accepted the new boat on behalf of the station and a service of dedication was then conducted by Revd Harry Burlton and Revd Howard Curnow. After a vote of thanks proposed by Mr Andrew Young, RNLI South West Regional Manager, the lifeboat was named by Colonel Tony Barnett and then launched for an exercise with a helicopter from 771 Squadron RNAS Culdrose.

The ILB is launched on a trolley which is hoisted onto the short slipway from its position beside the lifeboat in the boathouse by hoist, which was originally a manually-operated chain block affair but was converted to electric power in 2001. When in position over the short slipway, the ILB and trolley are lowered onto the slipway. The weight of the rig is then taken by tensioning the winch wire so that

D Class inflatable inshore lifeboat D-490 *Spirit of the ACC* on exercise. (Tim Stevens)

The scene on the beach at Sennen Cove on 30 June 1996 during the naming ceremony of D-490 *Spirit of the ACC*. (Paul Richards)

After the naming ceremony of D-490 *Spirit of the ACC* on 30 June 1996, standing behind the new boat are left to right, back row: Andrew Prowse, Trevor Beckwith, Neil Willis. Front row, Tim Nicholas, Andrew Tonkin, Daniel Shannon. (Tim Stevens)

the lifting strops can be removed. On the instruction of the helmsman, the ILB is lowered down the short slipway and into the water. At low tide the ILB is lowered down the short slip to its foot and then manually pushed into the water, a difficult task at big spring tides as ILB and trolley have to be pushed over rocks in the harbour. The winch originally used for lowering the trolley down the slipway was a petrol driven capstan on a small trolley which was set in a frame secured to the boathouse floor. The trolley was lowered and winched up on a rope. Just before the

D-490 *Spirit of the ACC* on exercise in the Bay
with RNAS Rescue Helicopter, July 1996.
(Paul Richards)

refurbishment of the station in 2001–02, a more powerful winch was installed which
was electrically operated and used a steel wire, proving to be a much efficient and
safer set-up.

During the boathouse refurbishment (described below), a temporary ILB house
was erected in the top of the car park. Using the winch to launch the ILB from this
site proved too difficult creating unnecessary hazards to both shore crew and public,
so a Land Rover was allocated to the station enabling the ILB to be towed down the
harbour slipway and into the sea with ease, causing minimal disruption to the public
and a much quicker response when called out on service.

While a complete list of ILB services can be found in the Appendix, the following
brief descriptions provide a year-by-year account of some of the work undertaken by
the station's D Class inflatable since it has been operated from Sennen. While the
typical services are fairly routine for the lifeboat's crew, the ILB provides a quick and
efficient safeguard for users of the seas off Land's End.

1996: five launches. The first service of the year took place on 31 May. D-490 was
launched at 3.47 p.m. after an urgent request to assist a surfer who was in trouble in
heavy surf off the beach. The surfer was rescued from the heavy surf and a lifeguard,
who had gone to help the casualty, was also brought ashore by the ILB. On 14 June,
D-490 assisted a small punt and its four occupants who were attempting to row back
to Sennen in adverse conditions. Two weeks later, on 31 July, she launched at 12.47 p.m.
to assist the Coastguard recover a badly injured man from Pednvounder Beach,
Porthcurno.

A dramatic photograph of D-490 *Spirit of the ACC* in the surf, typical of the kind of difficult conditions in which she has often been tasked to work. (Tim Stevens)

1997: eleven launches. During a busy year for the ILB, the relief D Class inflatable D-425 *Strickson* was on station from 16 April until 10 September. On 28 May she launched to investigate a diver's float near Cowloe Rocks, Sennen, and recovered an abandoned float. On 29 June she was launched at 4.15 a.m. with the all-weather lifeboat to assist the yacht *Boucanier* ashore near Nanquidno. One person was rescued from the yacht which was subsequently refloated on the tide and towed to Newlyn by *The Four Boys*. After two false alarms in August, on 6 September, D-425 was launched in the early evening to assist in the recovery of a cliff faller at Logan Rock, Porthcurno. On 26 September, the crew of the relief D Class recovered a body from the sea at Folly Cove and the following day launched again to search for missing person at Land's End. The lifeboatmen sighted a body at the foot of a cliff and it was subsequently recovered by helicopter. The final launch of the year took place on 24 November: D-490, back on station, launched at 4.02 p.m. to a surfer off Sennen beach and rescued the man who had been in trouble.

1998: seven launches. On 24 March, D-490 launched on service at 12.15 p.m. and rescued three youngsters cut off by the tide at Aire Point. Just over a month later, on 28 April, she was launched at 1.10 p.m. and saved a surfer who was in difficulties in Sennen Bay. During May and July she carried out two fruitless searches and undertook another search on 4 August for a missing person who was eventually located safe and well at home. Two days later, D-490 launched at 6.47 p.m. following a report that some persons were in the water between the Brisons and Carn Gloose. After arriving on the scene, the ILB picked two divers out of the water and reunited

D Class inflatable D-490 *Spirit of the ACC* during a first aid exercise at Pendeen in April 1998. (Tim Stevens)

them with their dive boat. The final service of the year, on 1 November, was performed after a partly submerged canoe had been spotted off Cape Cornwall. The remains of the canoe were recovered and brought back to Sennen Cove but no one was reported missing. From 18 November 1998 until 24 February 1999 the relief D-412 *BP Service* was on station in place of D-490.

1999: eleven launches. The first service of the year was undertaken in force four to five wind and a moderate swell. D-490 launched at 3.42 p.m. on 5 April to assist a surfer caught in a rip tide off Sennen Beach, ensuring he reached the beach safely. In May the ILB's speed and agility proved essential in saving the life of an injured person, with the skills of her crew proving equally crucial during this service. At 12.50 p.m. on 30 May, D-490 was launched to assist a person who had fallen over the cliffs at Ped–Men–Du, to the west of Sennen Cove. Crew members Tim Nicholas and Colin Brown were landed at the cliffs and administered first aid to the casualty, who had a leg injured and suspected neck and back injuries. The casualty was airlifted to Treliske Hospital by helicopter and the ILB returned to station at 2.12 p.m. As a result of their first-aid actions during this service, Nicholas and Brown received letters of commendation from the RNLI.

D-490 was called out three times in August, assisting a windsurfer, searching after a report of a red flare and assisting the all-weather lifeboat by bringing ashore a sick crew member from a yacht that the lifeboat was towing. D-490 was called on twice

on 10 August, first to assist a sailing dinghy with two persons on board and then to help with a search for a missing person at Land's End. On 26 August, D-490 was launched at 10.51 a.m. to investigate reports of two persons in the water near Shark's Fin Rock, off Land's End. They proved to be crew from the Sennen fishing boat *Boy Matt* and were rescued by helicopter while the ILB assisted in recovering the fishing boat which had been swamped by a large wave approximately two hours previously.

2000: one service. D-490 was launched on 20 July to investigate a report of abandoned clothing at Porthcurno. However, nothing was found and no-one was reported missing so the ILB returned to station after what proved to be the only service of the year.

2001: seven launches. The first launch of the year, on 15 April, proved to be a false alarm with good intent. The dangers of the surf and currents off Sennen were apparent on 25 May when D-490 was launched at 2.50 p.m. to assist four swimmers in trouble off Sennen beach in a moderate surf and tide rip. Two swimmers were recovered by the ILB, with a further two being rescued by lifeboat crew members who went to their aid from the beach. From 22 June until 23 October, relief D Class inflatable D-467 *Kathleen Scadden* was on station and she was launched four times during August. On 19 August she went to assist two swimmers reported in trouble off Sennen beach. The next day she assisted canoeists in trouble in the strong current in the Tribbens channel to the west of the Cove. One canoeist was rescued by the ILB and brought ashore while the other two reached shore safely. On 26 August, D-467 rescued two swimmers to the west of Sennen Beach who were being carried away by a combination of the wind and tide and had become exhausted. Two days later she went out with the all-weather lifeboat at 9.30 a.m. to check on the safety of the Sennen Cove fishing boat *Polpry* which was located and found not to be in need of assistance.

2002: nine launches. On 28 March, D-490 was launched to assist three divers who were unable to swim against the strong easterly wind. The casualties were recovered and brought back to Sennen. On 28 May D-490 was called out in the dark to assist

At the station's Annual Dinner in March 2000, RNLI Area Organizer Andrew Young presents Colin Brown and Tim Nicholas (to right) with letters of commendation for their efforts during a combined service in May 1999 with the Land's End Cliff Rescue team and an RNAS Culdrose helicopter. Their award recognized the high standard of first aid and care demonstrated during the rescue. (Tim Stevens)

During the rebuilding of the lifeboat house in 2001, the ILB was kept in this temporary house and was launched over the beach using a Land Rover. (Tim Stevens)

Land Rover LR36 launches relief D Class inflatable D-467 *Kathleen Scadden* down the stone slipway and across the beach on exercise during summer 2001. (Tim Stevens)

Capsize exercise with D-367 *Seahorse* (ex-Trearddur Bay), an old D Class inflatable supplied specifically to enable the ILB crew to practise capsize drills such as this. (Tim Stevens)

D-490 *Spirit of the ACC*, on her trolley, is winched back into the boathouse via the specially-installed overhead gantry used to position her on the short slipway for launching. (Nicholas Leach)

the drilling rig just off the lifeboat station ashore. The ILB set out at 10 p.m. into a rough sea with a heavy current and returned twenty minutes later with the rig's crew. After two launches in July, on 12 August D-490 was launched at 7 a.m. to assist a surfer thought to be in difficulties off Sennen Beach. The casualty, who was tired and unable to regain the shore, was safely landed at the lifeboat station and the ILB was recovered fifteen minutes after launching. Three days later, D-490 assisted a small dinghy with engine failure in Sennen Bay, bringing the dinghy and its occupant safely back to the Cove.

A station for the twenty-first century

The development of new and larger lifeboat houses at Sennen Cove began during the 1890s when a new house was built on the present location (see end of Chapter 2). The boathouse was considerably enlarged and rebuilt in 1929 incorporating two slipways for launching and recovery as well as a turntable inside the house to enable a bow recovery in an attempt to overcome the problems of launching at all states of the tide across the Cove's rocky beach. The turntable was used to turn the lifeboat through 360 degrees so that it could be aligned with either slipway as necessary. The turntable and double slipway were features unique to Sennen and meant that the boathouse itself was the biggest in the British Isles. This building remained much the

same until 1991; since then, however, it has been adapted and improved on several occasions to meet the needs of a modern lifeboat crew in the twenty-first century.

The shoreworks of 1991 involved converting the house so that the 12m Mersey *The Four Boys* could be accommodated. The doors were raised to give the necessary clearance for the new boat and the slipways were both refurbished, a task which involved stripping the existing steelwork, encasing the original structure with reinforced concrete and building a new slipway platform/keelway to fit the profile of the Mersey. In addition, a public viewing gallery was provided above the winches. While the changes were taking place, the relief Rother *Harold Salvesen* on station had to operate from a mooring. The majority of the work was carried out by Tarmac while the viewing gallery was built in early 1992 by Symons Construction.

Following the allocation of the 47ft Tyne during the mid-1990s, further alterations were needed to ensure the new boat could be operated successfully. A system of hydraulics was fitted to the turntable while movement of the turntable was restricted to between the two slipways as, despite the size of the boathouse, the 47ft boat was too large to turn through a full 360 degrees. A few months before the Tyne arrived, the steel beams in the boathouse roof were altered to increase headroom. The slipways and turntable had to be altered again: hardwood timbers were placed on them to make up the difference in depth of the bilge keels between the two classes of boat. Work began a couple of weeks before the changeover, starting at the short slipway, moving on to the turntable and finishing with the top of the short slipway. As each area was altered, it became unusable for the Mersey which was eventually restricted to the long slipway. She remained here until her final launch on 5 December 1998. When the Tyne was placed on station, timbers were fixed to the long slipway thus preventing a Mersey from coming to Sennen again without the alterations being reversed.

The 12m Mersey *The Four Boys* on the turntable inside the lifeboat house in the summer of 1996, giving a good indication of the interior of the building before it was refurbished and renewed five years later. (Peter Edey)

The lifeboat house and slipways with Rother *Diana White* on the long slipway. The remains of the launchway built in 1919 for the trolley and rail operation can be seen between the two slipways. (Peter Barnfield)

The lifeboat house and slipways as adapted for 12m Mersey. (Nicholas Leach)

With the arrival in 1998 of a Tyne at the station, large areas of space became available inside the boathouse. This space had been needed previously for turning the lifeboat through a full circle but, as this practise had ceased, the space could now be utilized more effectively to provide improved accommodation for the crew and their gear. In September 2000, work started on a major refurbishment. While the changes were being made, the station operated from temporary accommodation in the nearby car park making use of portable buildings for changing rooms, stores and a crew room.

The ILB was also housed at this location and *Spirit of the ACC* was launched down the harbour slip by Land Rover. The lifeboat was placed on the top of the long

12m Mersey *The Four Boys* at the head of the long slipway while the launching arrangements were adapted for the 47ft Tyne. (Phil Weeks)

slipway to avoid damage from building debris but remained in complete readiness for service. The winches, turntable and both slipways were fully operational as building work continued around them.

The refurbished building was designed so that the next generation of slipway-launched lifeboat could be accommodated. The multiple gable-ended roof was dismantled and a new shallow-arched steel structure put in its place with the height of the wall plate raised by approximately one metre. This extra height, together with the widening of the doors, provides sufficient room to accommodate a new Tamar-class fast-slipway lifeboat. Internally, the previous crew facilities and workshop were removed to provide space for a new three-storey structure consisting of a ground floor ILB changing room, a first floor lifeboat changing room with access through double doors straight out on to the lifeboat's starboard deck, and a crew room on the second floor. On the opposite side of the building, a high level fuelling gantry was constructed together with a walkway to the port side deck of the ALB. Below this, a workshop, rope store and cleaning area for the shore crew were built.

The lifeboat station was due to be completed by Easter 2001 but, due to various delays, was not finished until the late summer. During the building work, the operational side went relatively smoothly although, following a service launch on 20 March 2001, *Norman Salvesen* had to be recovered on the long slip in total darkness and an easterly gale as the temporary slipway lighting had failed. Conditions prevented the shore crew from carrying out the normal rigging of recovery ropes so, with careful manoeuvring in the narrow channel, the lifeboat crew had to rig their own recovery lines as they veered back onto the slip – quite an achievement in such a tight space and in such conditions.

The new house was formally opened at a ceremony on 16 February 2002. Adrian Semmens, Chairman of the station, welcomed guests and Air Vice Marshal J.F.H. Tetley, CB, CVO, Deputy Chairman of the RNLI, accepted the refurbished lifeboat house, handing it over into the care of the honorary secretary, John Chappell. At the invitation of the honorary secretary, George Rawlinson, Staff Officer (Divisions) formally reopened the boathouse. A service of dedication, conducted by Revd Harry Burton, Vicar of Sennen, followed and a vote of thanks, proposed by Simon Pryce, Divisional Inspector of Lifeboats, completed the ceremony.

However, although the boathouse improvements were complete, the launching channel needed to be made both deeper and wider. This work, which commenced in March 2002, was necessary to increase the safety margin, particularly in the two hours before low water when a strong current runs across the channel with a danger that the lifeboat could be swept ashore while manoeuvring at slow speed in the channel. A digger mounted on a walking rig together with a forty-ton long-reach swing shovel operating from the shore when tides permitted combined to carry out the necessary work. The rig was on site until early September 2002 and the whole operation was successfully completed. Over 8,600 tons of spoil were removed and taken up over Cove Hill by dumper trucks pulled by tractors. As a result of these improvements, the Sennen Cove lifeboat station now has a modern, spacious lifeboat house ready to meet the challenges of the twenty-first century. And the problems of launching and recovery – that made operations so difficult – have largely been overcome. In the 150 years that the station has been open, Sennen Cove lifeboats have launched 544 times and saved the lives of 389 people.

47ft Tyne *Norman Salvesen* is recovered stern first up the short slipway after exercise, April 1999. The changes to accommodate her in the boathouse meant that she had to be recovered stern first, as at all other RNLI slipway stations, but unlike Sennen lifeboats hitherto. This photograph shows the boat reversing onto the toe of the slipway ready to be hauled clear of the water by the winch in the boathouse once the wire cable has been attached. (Tim Stevens)

The boathouse without a roof in November 2000 during the extensive refurbishment, with 47ft Tyne *Norman Salvesen* ready for service at the head of the long slipway. (Tim Stevens)

The support beams of the roof in place with 47ft Tyne *Norman Salvesen* on the launching cradle at the head of the slipway as refurbishment work continues around her, January 2001. (Tim Stevens)

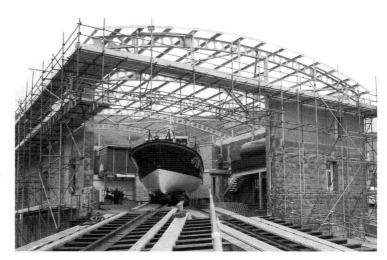

The curved roof in place as the refurbishment work is gradually completed during spring 2001. (Tim Stevens)

By June 2001, work on the boathouse was almost completed but new doors had yet to be supplied, and finishing of the interior was under way. (Tim Stevens)

The refurbished lifeboat house, with a shallow-arched steel roof and both 47ft Tyne and D Class inflatable on the slipways. (Nicholas Leach)

The Sea Core Rig in position off the slipway to work on improving the launching channel, with the all-weather lifeboat on moorings while the work was undertaken, 2002. (Tim Stevens)

Appendix 1. Lifeboat summary

On station	ON	Name Donor	Type Year built	Launches/ lives saved
1853–64	—	(Not named) RNLI Funds	25'8" Self-righter 1853	1/0
1864–80	—	*Cousins William and Mary Ann of Bideford* Gift Mrs M.A. Davis, Bideford	33' Self-righter 1864	2/2
1880–93	182	*Denzil and Maria Onslow* Gift Miss Maria Onslow, Faygate	34' Self-righter 1880	5/10
1893–1922	357	*Ann Newbon* Legacy Robert Alger Newbon, Islington	35' Self-righter 1893	75/132
1922–48	674	*The Newbons* Legacy Robert Alger Newbon, Islington	40' Self-righter (M) 1922	54/36
1948–73	856	*Susan Ashley* Legacy of Charles Carr Ashley, France	41' Watson (M) 1948	87/64
1974–91	999	*Diana White* An anonymous gift and part of the Cornish Lifeboat Appeal	37'6" Rother (M) 1973	80/63
1991–98	1176	*The Four Boys* Land's End Lifeboat Appeal, plus others	12m Mersey (M) 1991	90/47
1998-	1121	*Norman Salvesen* Bequest of Mrs Mary 'Mickie' Salvesen	47ft Tyne (M) 1988	

(M) indicates motor lifeboat   (TSD) indicates Temporary Station Duty

Inshore lifeboats

3.1994	D-365	— —	16'3" Avon EA16	
1994	D-450	*Anthony* —	16'3" Avon EA16	
1995	D-448	*Sea Ranger* —	16'3" Avon EA16	
30.3.1996–	D-490	*Spirit of the ACC* The Royal Logistic Corps and others	16'3" Avon EA16	

Appendix 2. Lifeboat detail

First lifeboat (not named)

Years on station	June 1853 – 1864
Donor	Provided out of RNLI Funds
Cost	£141
Type	Peake self-righter, six-oared
Year built	1853
Builder	Forrestt, Limehouse
Dimensions	25ft x 6ft 8in x 3ft 2in
Weight	1 ton 8 cwt
Disposal	Broken up 1864

Cousins William and Mary Ann of Bideford

Years on station	July 1864 – August 1880
Donor	Gift of Mrs Mary Ann Davis, Bideford
Cost	£250
Type	Self-righter, ten-oared
Year built	1864
Builder	Forrestt, Limehouse
Dimensions	33ft x 8ft
Weight	3 tons
Disposal	Damaged on service at various times, broken up 1880

Denzil and Maria Onslow

Years on station	August 1880 – July 1893
Donor	Gift of Miss Maria Onslow, Staughton House, St Neot's, in memory of her late brother
Naming ceremony	Publicly launched on 20 August 1880 at Penzance
Cost	£363
Official Number	182
Type	Self-righter, ten-oared, double-banked
Year built	1880
Builder	Woolfe, Shadwell
Dimensions	34ft x 8ft 3in x 4ft 3in
Disposal	Broken up 1893

Ann Newbon

Years on station	20 July 1893 – May 1922
Donor	Legacy of Robert Alger Newbon, Islington
Cost	£498 2s 0d
Official Number	357
Type	Self-righter, ten-oared
Year built	1893
Builder	Woolfe, Shadwell, yard no. W 255
Dimensions	35ft x 8ft 3in x 4ft 2in
Weight	3 tons 16 cwt
Disposal	Condemned May 1922 after being found defective, dismantled for sale at Newlyn, sold 24 July 1922 for £22. Subsequent whereabouts unknown.

The Newbons

Years on station	1 May 1922 – July 1948
Donor	Legacy of Robert Alger Newbon, Islington, London
Naming ceremony	Named on 28 August 1924
Cost	£8622 4s 9d
Official Number	674
Type	Motor self-righter, single screw
Year built	1922
Builder	J.S. White, East Cowes, yard no. W 1576
Dimensions	40ft x 10ft 6in x 5ft 10in
Weight	11 tons 16 cwt, later 12 tons 16 cwt
Notes	Left Cowes 28.4.1922 and arrived at Sennen on 1.5.1922; the 226m journey was undertaken in 30 hours at sea. Overhauled and stored at J. S. White's, Cowes, from 22.6.1928 to 25.7.1929 during the rebuilding of the lifeboat house.
Disposal	Sold out of service on 7 March 1951 to W. Morris Wooding & Miss J.I. Fitchett, Warrington. Renamed *Fair Lady,* she was converted in 1965 at Carnarvon and was in use as a fishing boat at Hoylake in 1969. She was later seen at Morpeth Dock, Birkenhead, converted into a yacht but her current whereabouts are not known.

Susan Ashley

Years on station	26 July 1948 – May 1973
Donor	Legacy of Charles Carr Ashley, Mentone, France
Naming ceremony	Was to be named on 4 Spetember 1948, but due to a service the previous night, after which the weather was too bad for rehousing, she was moored at Newlyn; here she remained until 5 September, and so was not present for her inaugural ceremony, which went ahead as planned except for the naming which then took place on 2 October 1948 when she was formally christened by Lady Burnett.
Cost	£13,357 2s 8d
Official Number	856
Type	Watson motor, twin screw
Year built	1948
Builder	Groves & Guttridge, Cowes, yard no. G&G 481
Dimensions	41ft x 11ft 8in
Weight	14 tons 16 cwt
Disposal	Sold 1980 to the National Lifeboat Museum, Bristol, whose entire collection, including *Susan Ashley,* was subsequently moved to Chatham Historic Dockyard. She has been displayed at Chatham since 1995.

Diana White

Years on station	1 November 1973 – 10 April 1991
Donor	An anonymous gift and part of the Cornish Lifeboat Appeal
Naming ceremony	Named on 19 July 1974 by HRH Duke of Kent
Cost	£89,000
Official Number	999
Type	Rother, twin screw
Year built	1973
Builder	William Osborne, Littlehampton, yard no. WO 20
Dimensions	37ft 6in x 11ft 6in x 5ft
Weight	12 tons 12 cwt
Disposal	Left Sennen Cove on 10 April 1991 and although still officially the station lifeboat until December, she did not return. During 1992 she was stored at the RNLI Depot, Poole, pending her sale to the Sumner Lifeboat Institution, New Zealand. In 1992, she was sold to Sumner Lifeboat Institution, New Zealand, and she served as a lifeboat until 1999. The Sumner Institution then sold her and she is now privately owned in the Bay of Plenty, New Zealand.

The Four Boys

Years on station	5 December 1991 – 2 December 1998
Donor	The Land's End Lifeboat Appeal, money raised by parents of the four Stoke Poges school boys lost off Land's End in May 1985, The London Broadcasting Company Appeal, the bequests of Clement Arthur Holland and Pattie Hiddleston, together with other gifts and legacies.
Naming ceremony	Named on 22 April 1992 by the Duke of Kent
Cost	£655,250
Official Number	1176
Type	Mersey, twin screw
Year built	1991
Builder	FBM Ltd, Cowes, yard no. 1284
Dimensions	38ft x 12ft 6in x 6ft
Notes	Arrived at Sennen on 28 November 1991 for slipway trials which lasted until 5 December, when she was officially placed on service. After service at Sennen, she took part in the 175th Anniversary Lifeboat Flotilla, Poole, on 22-23 June 1999. She was then reallocated to Amble where she arrived on 8 July 1999. She was rededicated on 13 May 2000 at Radcliffe Quay, Amble, by the Reverend Janet Brearley, Vicar of Warkworth with Acklington.

Norman Salvesen

Years on station	3 December 1998 –
Donor	Bequest of the late Mrs Mary 'Mickie' Salvesen.
Naming ceremony	Named on 16 September 1988 at The North Pier, Harbour, Wick, by Mrs Bright Gordon, MBE, after the donor's husband
Cost	£566,124
Official Number	1121
Type	Tyne, twin screw
Year built	1988
Builder	Hull built by Wright, Derby; fitted out by Harrison, Amble
Dimensions	47ft x 15ft
Weight	25 tons 8 cwt
Notes	Stationed at Wick from 1988 to 1998, originally slipway launched, but from 1994 kept moored afloat in Wick Harbour. After service at Wick, she was refitted and left Poole on 26 November 1998 for Sennen, travelling via Alderney, St Peter Port, Fowey, St Mary's, Sennen, and she arrived at Newlyn Harbour on 29 November 1998. Rededicated on 29 June 1999 by the Revd Harry Burlton, Rector of St Buryan, St Sennen and St Levan.

47ft Tyne *Norman Salvesen* was placed on station at Sennen Cove on 5 December 1998. (Tim Stevens)

Appendix 3. Service summary

First Lifeboat

1856 May 6-7 Barque *Charles Adolphe*, of La
Rochelle, assisted to save vessel

Cousins William and Mary Ann of Bideford Lifeboat

1865 Oct 13 Longships lighthouse, landed a
keeper seriously ill, saved 1

1868 Oct 23 Government lighter *Devon*, saved 1

Denzil and Maria Onslow Lifeboat

1883 Jan 8 Cutter *Spring*, of Guernsey, saved
vessel and 3

1889 Oct 15 Steamship *Malta*, of Glasgow,
rendered assistance and saved 7

Ann Newbon Lifeboat

1894 Dec 24 HMS *Lynx*, rendered assistance

1895 Oct 17 Steamship *Harberton*, of London,
assisted to save vessel

1898 Nov 10 Steamship *Blue Jacket*, of Cardiff,
saved 22

1901 Oct 21 2 fishing boats of Sennen Cove,
landed 5

Nov 18 Schooner *Mary James*, of Penzance,
saved 6

1902 May 27 HMS *Recruit*, stood by

1903 Feb 4 Boat of steamship *Benwick*, of
Newcastle, saved 5

1908 Dec 29 Ship *Fairport*, of Liverpool, assisted
to save vessel and 20

1910 Mar 13 Trawler *Harry*, of Brixham, saved
trawler's boat and 4

1912 Feb 29 Steamship *Northlands*, of Cardiff,
stood by

Mar 14 Trawler *Condor*, of Brixham, stood by

1913 Apr 4 Ketch *Woolwich Infant*, of Falmouth,
stood by

Aug 14 Steamship *J. Duncan*, of Cardif,
landed 2 and saved 12

1917 Feb 20 HM Seaplane, saved 1

Apr 20 Steamship *Polyktor*, of Ithaca, saved 28

Sep 10 Steamship *Ioanna*, of London, landed 3

1918 Feb 7 Steamship *Beaumaris*, of London,
stood by, rendered assistance and
saved 18

1919 Mar 17 Steamship *Falmouth Castle*, of
Falmouth, landed 7

Apr 29 Boat of steamship *Frisia*, of
Rotterdam, saved 14

Nov 30 HM Motor launch 378, saved 8

1920 Sep 22 Motor fishing boat *Our Boys*, of
Porthleven, saved 5

1921 Jan 22 Steamship *Haliartus*, of Liverpool,
assisted to save vessel

Aug 16 Barge *Strumble*, of London, saved vessel

The Newbons Lifeboat

1923 Sep 29 Steamship *Gutfeld*, of Hamburg,
rendered assistance

Oct 8 Steamship *City of Westminster*, of
Liverpool, saved 13

1926 Mar 20 Schooner *Ada*, of Barrow, assisted to
save vessel and 6

Apr 20 Steamship *Deansway*, of Cardiff,
stood by

1931 Aug 29 A small boat of Priest's Cove, saved
boat and 3

1934 July 15 Fishing ketch *Replete*, of Brixham,
landed 4

1936 Feb 10 Boat of ketch *Albatros*, of Brest,
saved a dog and 4

Dec 21 Steamship *Mina*, of Parnu, rendered
assistance and stood by

1937 Feb 16 Steamship *Svanhild*, of Elsinore,
stood by

1938 Dec 18 Schooner *Bretonne*, of Treguier, saved 5

1942 Sep 12 Aeroplane in sea, salved wreckage

Oct 8 Aeroplane, picked up 2 bodies, and
salved rubber dinghy

1944 June 30 US Army Motor Launch MT.392,
saved launch

1945 Jan 21 Steamship *George Hawley*, of
Savannah, Georgia, USA, saved 5

Feb 24 Unknown vessel, torpedoed,
wreckage found

Mar 22 Steamship *Empire Kingsley*, of
Greenock, landed 49

Mar 29 HM Frigate *Teme*, of Royal Canadian
Navy, rendered assistance, stood by

Susan Ashley Lifeboat

1948 Oct 11 Steamship *Woodlark*, of London, gave
help and transferred 1 survivor of
the fishing boat *Saphir*, of
Camaret, to another craft

Oct 26 Ex-War Department hulk *Empire
Flamingo*, saved 4

1952 Jan 6 Took doctors and a nurse to Scilly,
thereby saving a life

July 20 Yacht *Morena*, of London, rendered
assistance

1953 Apr 18 Yacht *Larry*, of Southampton, saved
yacht and 3

1956 July 30 Yacht *Westo II*, of Southampton,
saved yacht

1961   June 28 French trawler *Enfant des Houles*,
                 rendered assistance
1962   May 9   Man trapped on cliff, landed a body
       July 9   Cabin cruiser *Eldora*, towed in cruiser
       July 28 Swimmers on rocks, saved 2
       Aug 4   Motor tug *Sally*, of Rochester,
                 rendered assistance
       Aug 25   Girl on rocks, landed a body

Edmund and Mary Robinson Reserve Lifeboat

1962   Nov 3   Trawler *Jeanne Gougy*, of Dieppe,
                 landed 2 bodies

Susan Ashley Lifeboat

1963   Sep 13   Motor vessel *Alacrity*, of London,
                 gave help and stood by
1964   Mar 24   Trawler *Victoire Roger*, of Ostend,
                 saved 5
1965   July 1   Motor boat *Wheal Geevor*, escorted
                 boat
       July 25 Motor boat *Marea*, saved boat and 4
       Sep 25   Motor fishing vessel *Spray*, of
                 Penzance, gave help
1966   Mar 30   German motor vessel *Hille
                 Oldendorft*, of Lübeck, landed
                 injured man
       July 21 2 youths cut off by tide, saved 2
       July 30 Motor launch *Kathleen*, escorted boat
                 and landed 1
1967   June 11 Motor cruiser *Potemkin*, saved boat
                 and 5
       June 20 Yacht *Tropacara*, saved boat and 2
       Aug 28   French trawler *Moguerie*, escorted
       Sep 12   Fishing boat *Onward*, gave help
1968   Apr 12   Exhibition *Galleon Hispaniola*, saved
                 boat and 4
       Apr 13   Sick man on Wolf Rock Lighthouse,
                 stood by
       Aug 23   3 persons washed off rocks, saved 3
1969   Apr 16   Yacht *Mahe*, of Faversham, saved
                 boat and 2
       Aug 2   2 boys cut off by the tide, stood by
                 for helicopter
       Aug 13   Trimaran *Blue Rose*, saved boat and 3
       Oct 10   Motor fishing vessel *Antelope*, saved
                 boat and 4
       Dec 30   Sevenstones Lightvessel, landed a sick
                 man
1970   July 16 Man fallen over cliff, and 2 men cut
                 off by tide, saved 3
1971   Jan 8   Motor fishing vessel *Aquilon*, of
                 Lorient, gave help
       June 8   Motor fishing vessel *T.G.S.* [PZ.96],
                 saved boat and 1
       Aug 9   2 persons stranded on rocks, assisted
                 to save 2

1972   Mar 23   Yacht *Dogwatch*, of Cowes, saved boat
                 and 1
       Aug 22   Motor boat, gave help
       Sep 7   Trawler *La Varenne*, of Cherbourg,
                 saved 8
       Sep 8   Yacht *Titatam*, saved boat and 2
       Sep 23   Yacht *Etam*, of Southampton, saved
                 boat and 3

Amelia Relief Lifeboat (on station 10.4.1973–31.12.1973)

1973   Apr 19   Tug *Platina*, in tow of tug Plato,
                 stood by vessels
       Aug 2   Motor fishing vessel *Harry Hotspur*,
                 recovered wreckage
       Aug 19   Rowing boat, saved boat and 2
       Aug 22   Motor fishing vessel *Boy Jan*, of
                 Penzance, gave help

Diana White Lifeboat

1974   Apr 15   Motor yacht *Macasu*, saved boat and 5
1976   June 8   Motor fishing vessel *Gillian Clair*,
                 gave help
       July 15 Motor fishing vessel *Cape Cornwall*,
                 of St Ives, gave help
       Aug 4   Motor fishing vessel *Karren Eirean*, of
                 St Ives, gave help
       Dec 5   Motor fishing vessel *Gweer-Chez-
                 Viari*, of France, escorted vessel
1977   June 11 Salvage vessel *Anniline*, of Leith,
                 saved boat and 2
       Aug 1   Motor fishing vessel *Western Home*, of
                 Penzance, gave help
       Nov 16   Coaster *Union Crystal*, assisted with
                 search

Vincent Nesfield Relief Lifeboat (on station 1.12.1977–16.4.1978)

1977   Dec 5   Trawler *Boston Sea Ranger*, of
                 Lowestoft, saved 3
1978   Feb 18   Catamaran *Floral Dancer*, of
                 Falmouth, saved boat and 3

Diana White Lifeboat

1978   Apr 18   Fishing boat *Sweet Sue*, escorted boat
       June 14 Motor fishing vessel *Deux Soeurs*, of
                 Penzance, saved 3
1979   Feb 16   Motor fishing vessel *Aurelin*, of
                 France, in tow of motor fishing
                 vessel *Toenvor*, escorted
       Aug 16   Cargo vessel *Fordonna*, gave help
       Aug 26   Yacht *Agapanthus III*, saved boat and 5
1980   Mar 4   Woman fallen over cliff, landed a
                 body
       May 9   Motor fishing vessel *Bernadette
                 Denise*, of Poole, landed 2
       Aug 2   Yacht *Philerise II*, saved boat and 4

Oct 14 Injured man on board tanker *Grey Fighter*, of London, took out doctor and landed an injured man

Oct 17 Trawler *Floralie*, of France, escorted

Oct 24 Maternity case on board cargo vessel *St Patrick*, of Wexford, took out doctor

Dec 28 Fishing vessel *Shere Carn*, of Penzance, gave help

1981 May 3 Yacht *Hidair*, of Barry Dock, saved boat and 6

Sep 1 Yacht *Pearl Quest*, of Portsmouth, saved boat and 1

Sep 19 Cargo vessel *Tungufoss*, of Iceland, saved 7

Vincent Nesfield Relief Lifeboat
(on station 22.10.1981–15.5.1982)

1981 Dec 28 Missing crewman of cargo vessel *Mark*, of Panama, recovered liferaft

Diana White Lifeboat

1982 June 17 Yacht *Greenburrow*, of Bosham, escorted boat

1983 Mar 7 Fishing vessel *Lady Owen*, of Penzance, gave help

Apr 2 Ferry *Armorique*, of France, took out doctor, landed 38 and a body

July 10 Sick youth on board sail training vessel *Merlin*, of Clyde, took out doctor and landed a sick youth

July 12 Fishing vessel *We'll Try*, of Penzance, gave help

July 13 Yacht *Leigh Mary*, of Dublin, gave help

1984 Feb 12 Fishing vessel *Fleur-De-Lys*, of Penzance, gave help

Fishing vessel *Fleur-De-Lys*, of Penzance, escorted vessel

1985 Mar 16 Fishing vessel *Burutu*, in tow of fishing vessel escorted vessels

Apr 17 Motor cruiser *My Haven*, gave help

May 18 Fishing boat *Sarah Jane*, saved 1

May 25 Fishing vessel *Cassiopia*, stood by vessel

1986 Feb 8 Yacht Lily of the *Valley*, recovered liferaft and saved 3

Aug 7 Yacht *Lowly Worm*, saved boat and 4

Sep 13 Catamaran *Joint Assets*, saved boat and 1

The Davys Family Relief Lifeboat
(on station 21.12.1986–7.4.1988)

1987 June 16 Sick man on board fishing vessel *Galwad-Y-Mor*, of Falmouth, took out doctor and landed sick man

Oct 11 Fishing vessel *Swordfish*, gave help

1988 Mar 14 Fishing vessel *J.B.*, of Brixham, escorted vessel

Mar 25 Cargo vessel *Retriever*, of Cyprus, escorted vessel

Diana White Lifeboat

1988 Apr 22 Yacht *Katy*, saved boat and 4

Apr 30 Yacht *Tia*, saved boat and 4

1989 Apr 3 Yacht *Legend*, of Salcombe, saved boat and 4

May 30 Fishing vessel *Confide*, of Penzance, gave help

June 28 Yacht *Cariad-Y-Mor*, saved boat and 2

July 23 Yacht *Huff*, of Arklow, gave help

Nov 22 Fishing vessel *Celtic Crusader*, escorted vessel

1990 Jan 10 Yacht *Short Wave*, escorted boat

May 26 Yacht *Tre-Viljor*, saved boat and 2

June 14 Yacht *Tudor Crest*, gave help

July 5 Yacht *Koo-She*, saved boat and 4

July 19 Cargo vessel *Rocquaine*, stood by vessel

July 20 Motor cruiser *Albatross*, gave help

Oct 21 Dinghy *Jedi 4*, saved boat and 2

Harold Salvesen Relief Lifeboat
(on station 9.4.1991–9.10.1991)

1991 Apr 15 Fishing vessel *Scarlet Thread*, gave help

May 4 Fishing vessel *La Belle Bretagne*, gave help

July 15 Yacht *Alioth III*, gave help

Aug 1 Body in sea, recovered body

Aug 27 Rubber dinghy, escorted boat

The Four Boys Lifeboat

1992 May 10 Fishing vessel *Gorah Lass*, in tow of St Ives Lifeboat, escorted

May 16 Yacht *Nyota*, gave help

May 29 Fishing boat *Barry Anne*, landed 1 and saved boat

June 17 Yacht *Syrena*, gave help

June 23 Fishing vessel *Emblem*, landed 2

July 21 Fishing vessel *Sea Breeze II*, gave help

July 24 Yacht *Skeaby-Ny-Tonn*, gave help

July 25 Rubber dinghy *Raven II*, saved boat and 5

July 31 Rubber dinghy, gave help

Sep 21 Fishing vessel *Stereden-Va-Bro*, gave help

Sep 26 Man cut off by the tide, saved 1

Nov 3 Yacht *Lady Jazz*, gave help

1993 Feb 19 Fishing vessel *Children's Friend*, escorted

Mar 4 Injured man on board yacht *El Animado*, gave help

May 16 Yacht *Ophelie*, saved boat and 2

July 5 Fishing vessel *Sheila Jan*, gave help

July 13 Fishing vessel *Sea Spray*, gave help

July 17 Fishing vessel *Barryann*, gave help

July 21 Yacht *Tiree*, gave help

Margaret Jean Relief Lifeboat (on station 23.8.1993–28.9.1993)

Sep 15 Yacht *La Madeleine*, gave help

The Four Boys Lifeboat

Dec 10 Fishing vessel *Ben Loyal*, saved vessel and 6

1994 Mar 30 Fishing vessel *Kalon Briez*, saved vessel and 4

Apr 21 Fishing boat *Barry Ann*, 1 person and craft brought in

June 23 Yacht *Tresmorn Maid*, 3 persons and craft brought in

June 24 Fishing vessel *Seeker*, saved vessel and 2

July 9 Rubber dinghy, saved boat and 4

Aug 4 Fishing vessel *Golden Hope*, of Petroc, 5 persons and craft brought in

Aug 8 Catamaran *Alias*, saved boat and 5

Aug 9 Yacht *Sterelen Moor*, saved boat and 2

Sep 9 Yacht *Mandalay*, escorted boat

Oct 6 Motor cruiser *Lena II*, 1 person and craft brought in

Dec 6 Fishing vessel *Julian Paul*, assisted to save vessel and 5

Dec 10 Fishing vessel *Sowenna*, saved vessel and 5

1995 Apr 21 Sick man onboard fish carrier *Korallovyy*, took out doctor and landed an injured man

Lifetime Care Relief Lifeboat (on station 27.4.1995–18.9.1995)

May 28 Fishing vessel *Julian Paul*, landed 4 and craft brought in

June 26 Speedboat *Scubado*, landed 3 and boat saved

Aug 3 Yacht *Klompen*, 4 persons and craft brought in

Aug 12 Motor boat *Buzzard*, 2 persons and craft brought in

The Four Boys Lifeboat

Nov 7 Cargo vessel *Crescence*, stood by vessel

Nov 13 Fishing vessel *Fulmar*, 1 person and craft brought in

Nov 29 Fishing vessel *Kalon Breiz*, landed 4 and craft brought in

Dec 5 Fishing vessel *Taraqqi*, landed 3 and craft brought in

Dec 15 Cargo vessel *Arklow Bay*, gave help
Fishing vessel *Cheryl Elizabeth*, gave help

Dec 19 Fishing vessel *Superb*, landed 2 and craft brought in

Dec 20 Liferaft to fishing vessel *Tudor Owen*, saved liferaft

1996 June 12 Fishing vessel *Jackie G*, 2 persons and craft brought in

June 27 Motor boat *Barbary T*, 4 persons and craft brought in

June 29 Motor cruiser *Zarzuela*, 2 persons and craft brought in

July 19 Sailing dinghy, craft brought in

Aug 24 Fishing vessel *Scarlet Thread*, 4 persons and craft brought in

1997 Feb 19 Cargo vessel *Inishfree*, stood by vessel

Feb 28 Fishing vessel *Broonleigh*, saved craft and 2

May 5 Cargo vessel *Boy One*, escorted craft

June 29 Fishing vessel *Virgo Lady*, saved craft and 2

Yacht *Boucanier*, saved craft and 1

July 26 Yacht *Charisma*, 4 people and craft brought in

Aug 3 Yacht *Rip Rap*, landed 2 and craft brought in

Sep 26 Body in sea, gave help

Sep 27 Missing person, stood by

1998 July 3 Motor boat *Cathryn*, 3 persons and craft brought in

Aug 12 Restored steam drifter *Feasible*, 4 persons and craft brought in

Sep 24 Motor boat *Tir-Na-Nog*, saved boat and 1

Mariners Friend Relief Lifeboat (on station 3.12.1998–21.1.1999)

No effective services

Norman Salvesen Lifeboat

1999 Mar 25 Sick man onboard tug *Christine*, gave help

May 2 Yacht *Skyla-B*, gave help

May 8 Fishing vessel *Scarlet Thread*, saved vessel and 4

June 6 Yacht *Oggi*, 4 persons and craft brought in

July 4 Motor cruiser *Prime Time*, escorted

July 11 Motor cruiser *Tezzera*, saved craft and 2

July 26 Yacht *Sirena*, escorted

The Famous Grouse Relief Lifeboat (on station 29.7.1999-20.8.1999)

Aug 6 Yacht *Callianeira*, 3 persons and craft brought in

Norman Salvesen Lifeboat

Aug 26 Fishing vessel *Boy Matt*, assisted to save craft

Sep 18 Yacht *Marisol*, 5 people and craft brought in

Sep 24 Cargo vessel *Marman*, stood by

2000 Jan 18 Angling boat *Proper Job*, assisted vessel and 3 people

The Famous Grouse Relief Lifeboat

Feb 24 Fishing vessel *Harvest Reaper*, escorted vessel

Feb 27 Veteran landing craft *Rhino*, escorted vessel

Voluntary Worker Relief Lifeboat

Apr 30 Yacht *Mercurial Spirit*, assisted vessel and 4 people

Norman Salvesen Lifeboat

May 29 Yacht *Mouflon*, assisted vessel and 4 people

Nov 30 Fishing vessel *Intuition*, escorted craft

Dec 2 Fishing vessel *Silver Harvester*, escorted craft

Dec 21 Cargo vessel *Jens R*, escorted craft

2001 Jan 25 Fishing vessel *Vagabond*, landed 5 and craft brought in

Apr 6 Yacht *Saturnin*, saved craft and 1

Apr 21 Merchant vessel *Harns*, stood by

May 6 Ex–fishing vessel *Our Louise*, 2 persons and craft brought in

June 24 Yacht *Questor*, 2 persons and craft brought in

June 29 Yacht *Schiehallion*, 2 persons and craft brought in

July 10 Person fallen from cliff, stood by

Aug 21 Cabin cruiser *Westward*, 2 persons and craft brought in

Sep 30 Fishing vessel *Le Vagabond De Mer*, landed 5 and craft brought in

Dec 7 Cabin cruiser *Alesund*, 2 persons and craft brought in

2002 Jan 11 French trawler, 5 persons and craft brought in

Apr 29 Cargo vessel *Emma Pline*, stood by

Owen and Anne Aisher Relief Lifeboat (on station 2.4.2002–)

June 8 Fishing vessel *Stereden Va Bro*, saved 4

Norman Salvesen Lifeboat

July 6 Fishing vessel *Prevail*, 1 person and craft brought in

July 24 Yacht *Deception,* 1 person and craft brought in

Dec 9 Coaster *Hikie*, stood by

Dec 10 Yacht *Mercurial Spirit*, 2 persons and craft brought in

Inshore Lifeboats

1994 June 18 Tender to yacht *Sea King*, saved boat

June 21 Penwith Council rescue boat, 2 persons and craft brought in Canoe, escorted boat

July 29 Rubber dinghy, 10 persons and craft brought in

Aug 9 Yacht *Sterelen Moor*, 2 persons brought in saved by another lifeboat

Aug 11 Dinghy, 2 persons and craft brought in

1995 Apr 20 Injured cliff climber, stood by

Oct 5 Injured man onboard fishing vessel *Girl Pamela*, injured man brought in

1996 May 31 Surfboard, saved 1

June 14 Rowing boat *Kittiwake*, landed 4 and craft brought in

July 31 Injured man at Pedenvounder Beach, gave help

1997 June 29 Yacht *Boucanier*, gave help

Sep 6 Woman fallen from cliffs, stood by

Sep 26 Body in sea, landed a body

Sep 27 Missing person, gave help

Nov 24 Surfboard, landed 1 and board brought in

1998 Mar 24 Youngsters cut off by tide, saved 3

Apr 28 Surfer in difficulties, saved 1

Aug 6 Divers spotted in water, saved 2

1999 Apr 5 Surfer caught in rip tide, gave help

Apr 30 Cliff faller, assisted to save 1

July 11 Windsurfer, saved board and 1

July 26 Sick crewmember on yacht *Sirena*, 1 person brought in

Aug 10 Sailing dinghy, landed 2 and craft brought in

Aug 26 Fishing vessel *Boy Matt,* assisted to save craft

2000 No effective services

2001 May 25 Four swimmers, assisted to save 2

June 30 Yacht *Schiehallion,* gave help

Aug 20 Person overboard from canoe, saved craft and 1

Canoe, escorted craft

Aug 26 2 swimmers in difficulty, landed 2

2002 Mar 28 Divers in difficulty, saved 3

May 28 Drilling rig, gave help

July 24 Punt, three persons and craft brought in

Aug 12 Windsurfer, landed 1

Aug 15 Dinghy, 1 person and craft brought in

Oct 23 3 youths trapped at cliffs, stood by

Services up to 31 December 2002.

Appendix 4. Personnel summary

Honorary Secretaries

James Trembath	1853–63
Capt T.H. Fellowes, RN	1863–66
Nicholas B. Downing	1866–74
John Mathews	1874–81
Frederick C. Matthews	1881–85
Col T.H. Cornish	1886–1931
G.H. Bennetts	1931–46
J.K. Bennetts	1946–58
A.O. Kernick	1958–63
Capt H.B. Harvey	1963–74
Capt Evan Watson	1974–84
Capt James Summerlee	1984–95
Dr R.F. Manser	1995–2000
John Chappell	2000–

Coxswains

Matthew Nicholas	1853–75
Matthew Nicholas	1875–92
Henry Nicholas	1892–1911
Thomas Henry Nicholas	1911–20
Thomas Pender	1920–44
Edward Nicholas	1944
Nathaniel George	1944–47
John Roberts	1947–59
Henry Nicholas	11.1959–67
Horace Eric Pengilly★	1967–78
Maurice Hutchens★	1978–4.90
Terence Ronald George★	3.4.1990–

★Appointed as joint Coxswain/Mechanic

2nd Coxswains

Matthew Nicholas	1853–75
Henry Nicholas	1875–92
Philip Nicholas	1892
Thomas Henry Nicholas	1892–1911
Thomas Pender	1911–20
Edward Nicholas	1920–44 (?)
Nathaniel George	1944
John Roberts	1944–47
Richard Penrose	1947–56
James Howard Nicholas	1956–63
Maurice Hutchens	1968–73
Leonard Peplow	1973–77
John Pender	1978–82
Bill Price	1982–92
John Pender	1992–99
Philip Shannon	2000–

Mechanics

Henry James	1922–28
Henry Nicholas	1928–59
Richard George, snr	1959–63
Horace Eric Pengilly★	1963–67

Tom Pender, Coxswain from 1920, who served on the station's last pulling and first motor lifeboats. (By courtesy of RNLI Sennen Cove)

Appendix 5. What became of the lifeboats?

Susan Ashley

After service, *Susan Ashley* was taken to Bristol in 1980 for display with a collection of other lifeboats, but moved in 1995 along with all the other lifeboats to Chatham Historic Dockyard where she is maintained by volunteers as a central exhibit. (Nicholas Leach)

Diana White

Sold out of service in 1992 to the Sumner Lifeboat Institution of New Zealand, *Diana White* was renamed *Joseph Day* and used as a lifeboat until 1999. (Supplied by Tim Stevens)

Diana White

After service with the Sumner Lifeboat Institution *Diana White* was sold into private ownership and her name reverted to *Diana White* although she remained in New Zealand. She was kept at Taurananga, Bay of Penty, and was used as a pleasure boat. (Supplied by Tim Stevens)

The Four Boys

Following her seven years at Sennen Cove, *The Four Boys* was reallocated to the Amble station in Northumberland. The photograph shows her in the river Coquet during the station's annual lifeboat day in August 2002. (Nicholas Leach)

Bibliography

Amodeo, Colin (Ed) (1998): *Rescue: The Sumner Community and its lifeboat service.*

Cameron, Ian (2002): *Riders of the Storm* (Weidenfeld & Nicholson).

Corin, John and Farr, Grahame (1983): *Penlee Lifeboat* (Penlee & Penzance Branch of the RNLI).

Corin, John (1985): *Sennen Cove and its Lifeboat* (Sennen Cove Branch of the RNLI).

Larn, Richard (1991): *Shipwrecks around Land's End* (Tor Mark Press, Penryn, Cornwall).

Noall, Cyril and Farr, Grahame (1965): *Wreck and Rescue round the Cornish Coast: The Story of the Land's End Lifeboats* (D. Bradford Barton Ltd, Truro).

Leach, Nicholas (2002): *The Fowey Lifeboats: An Illustrated History* (Tempus Publishing, Stroud).

Sagar-Fenton, Michael (1991): *Penlee – The Loss of a Lifeboat* (Bossiney Books, Bodmin, Cornwall).

Warner, Oliver (1974): *The Lifeboat Service* (Cassell, London).

Woodman, Richard and Wilson, Jane (2002): *The Lighthouses of Trinity House* (Thomas Reed Publications, Bradford on Avon, Wilts).